Praise for Hilton Als's THE WOMEN

A truly subversive romance, *The Women* sets my mind and memory spinning. Each sentence cuts against expectation. No pieties hinder Hilton Als—a genius ashamed of nothing. This is a phenomenally glamorous book: read it slowly, then pass it to a fellow conspirator.

—Wayne Koestenbaum, author of *The Queen's Throat*

An antidote for much of the ill reason passed off as thought, Als' book, because of his caring attentions to minds "attracted to self-expression as it is filtered through an elliptical thought process," his "desultory interest in fact" and "profound interest in what the imagination can do," has many ramifications . . . This tender and brave book, whose scope is "life in this common world," is made up of beautiful sentences and paragraphs, balm.

—Bruce Hainley, *Artforum*

[Hilton Als] has put together three essays in *The Women*, all of them elliptical reflections on race, sexuality and identity that defy easy description. They are inventive and daring. They take up arms against cant and cliché . . . There is no doubt that they represent a fascinating sensibility. —Richard Bernstein, *The New York Times*

A stunning study of three people who turned conventional ideas of color, gender, and sexuality upside down in order to survive and shine. Even at their most unnerving, these are my new best friends, and Als—who writes with a painterly passion and a poet's grace—is my favorite Negress of them all. —Michael Musto

THE
WOMEN

THE
WOMEN

HILTON ALS

A DIVISION OF FARRAR, STRAUS AND GIROUX

NEW YORK

The Noonday Press
A division of Farrar, Straus and Giroux
19 Union Square West, New York 10003

Printed in the United States of America
Designed by Jonathan D. Lippincott
First published in 1996 by Farrar, Straus and Giroux

Portions of this work appeared in *The New Yorker* and *Grand Street* in different forms

The Library of Congress has catalogued the hardcover edition as follows:
Als, Hilton.
    The women / Hilton Als.
      p. cm.
    ISBN 0-374-52529-3
    1. American literature—Afro-American authors—History and criticism—Theory, etc.   2. Women and literature—United States—History—20th century.   3. Afro-Americans—Intellectual life.   4. Afro-American women—Biography.   5. Gender identity—United States.   6. Afro-Americans—Race identity.   7. Authorship—Sex differences.   8. Identity (Psychology)   I. Title.
PS153.N5A44   1996
810.9'896073'082—dc20   96–18360

This book is for my mother, Marie, and Kevin Ward Robbins; it is also for Darryl Turner and Moira Hodgson—all of whom are present

Grateful acknowledgment is made to three women in particular:
Brenda Phipps, Jean Stein, and Deborah Treisman

En route to la Côte Basque, Ahmet [Ertegun, then President of Atlantic Records] said, "I think there is a certain kind of rhythm and blues that will disappear, you know? 'Got My Mojo Workin',' and so forth. Black people are very ruthless about their own music. Wilson Pickett has one of the great voices, you know? One of the great *rough* rhythm-and-blues voices. But it is a little old-fashioned as far as black people are concerned. I like it, you like it, but a lot of black people have had enough." Ahmet continued, "R&B music can be very artificial. You know, very repetitive. I would say that at this moment R&B music is very artificial, with a lot of white influence, you know? And very insipid. R&B records can be very insipid. 'Hi, everybody,' you know? 'I'm Archie Bell & the Drells,' and so on and so forth. 'And we're gonna dance awhile,' and so forth, right?"

—GEORGE W. S. TROW
"Within the Context of No Context"

THE
WOMEN

1

Until the end, my mother never discussed her way of being. She avoided explaining the impetus behind her emigration from Barbados to Manhattan. She avoided explaining that she had not been motivated by the same desire for personal gain and opportunity that drove most female immigrants. She avoided recounting the fact that she had emigrated to America to follow the man who eventually became my father, and whom she had known in his previous incarnation as her first and only husband's closest friend. She avoided explaining how she had left her husband—by whom she had two daughters—after he returned to Barbados from England and the Second World War addicted to morphine. She was silent about the fact that, having been married once, she refused to marry again. She avoided explaining that my father, who had grown up relatively rich in Barbados and whom she had known as a child, remained a child and emigrated to America with his mother and his two sisters—women whose home he never left. She never mentioned that she had been attracted to my father's beauty and wealth partially because those were two things she would never know. She never discussed how she had visited my father in his room at night, and afterward crept down the stairs stealthily to return to her own home and her six children, four of them produced by her union with my father, who remained a child. She never explained that my father never went to her; she went to him. She avoided explaining that my father, like most children, and like most men, resented his children—four girls, two boys—for not growing up quickly enough so that they would leave home and take his responsibility away with them. She avoided recounting how my father—because he was a child—tried to distance himself from his children and his resentment of them through his derisive humor, teasing them to the point of cruelty; she also avoided recounting how her children, in order to shield themselves against the spittle of his derisive humor, absented themselves in his presence and, eventually, in the presence of any form of entertainment deliberately aimed at provoking laughter. She avoided explaining that in response to this resentment, my father also vaunted his beauty and wealth over his children, as qualities they would never share. She was silent about the mysterious bond she and my father shared, a bond so deep and volatile that their children felt forever diminished by their love, and forever compelled to disrupt, disapprove, avoid, or try to become a part of the love shared between any couple (specifically men and women) since part of our birthright has been to remain children, not unlike our father. She avoided mentioning the fact that my father had

other women, other families, in cities such as Miami and
Boston, cities my father roamed like a bewildered child.
She was silent about the fact that my father's mother and
sisters told her about the other women and children my
father had, probably as a test to see how much my mother
could stand to hear about my father, whom his mother
and sisters felt only they could understand and love, which
is one reason my father remained a child. My mother
avoided mentioning the fact that her mother, in Barbados,
had had a child with a man other than my mother's father,
and that man had been beautiful and relatively rich. She
avoided explaining how her mother had thought her association with that relatively rich and beautiful man would
make her beautiful and rich also. She avoided explaining
how, after that had not happened for her mother, her
mother became bitter about this and other things for the
rest of her very long life. She avoided contradicting her
mother when she said things like "Don't play in the sun.
You are black enough," which is what my grandmother
said to me once. She avoided explaining that she had
wanted to be different from her mother. She avoided explaining that she created a position of power for herself
in this common world by being a mother to children, and
childlike men, as she attempted to separate from her parents and siblings by being "nice," an attitude they could
never understand, since they weren't. She avoided recounting memories of her family's cruelty, one instance of their
cruelty being: my mother's family sitting in a chartered bus
as it rained outside on a family picnic; my mother, alone,
in the rain, cleaning up the family picnic as my mother's
aunt said, in her thick Bajun accent: "Marie is one of

God's own," and the bus rocking with derisive laughter as my heart broke, in silence. She avoided mentioning that she saw and understood where my fascination with certain aspects of her narrative—her emigration, her love, her kindness—would take me, a boy of seven, or eight, or ten: to the dark crawl space behind her closet, where I put on her hosiery one leg at a time, my heart racing, and, over those hose, my jeans and sneakers, so that I could have her—what I so admired and coveted—near me, always.

By now, the Negress has come to mean many things. She is perceived less as a mind than as an emotional being. In the popular imagination, she lives one or several cliché-ridden narratives. One narrative: she is generally colored, female, and a single mother, reduced by circumstances to tireless depression and public "aid," working off the books in one low-paying job after another in an attempt to support her children—children she should not have had, according to tax-paying, law-abiding public consensus. Like my mother. Another narrative: she can be defined as a romantic wedded to despair, since she has little time or inclination to dissemble where she stands in America's social welfare system, which regards her as a statistic, part of the world's rapacious silent majority. Like my mother. Another narrative: she gives birth to children who grow up to be lawless; she loves men who leave her for other women; she is subject to depression and illness. Her depression is so numbing that she rarely lets news of the outside world (television news, radio news, newspapers) enter her sphere of consciousness, since much of her time is spent fording herself and her children against the news of emotional disaster she sees day after day in the adult faces surrounding the faces of her children, who, in turn, look to her to make sense of it all. Like my mother.

What the Negress has always been: a symbol of America's by now forgotten strain of puritanical selflessness. The Negress is a perennial source of "news" and interesting "copy" in the newspapers and magazines she does not read because she is a formidable character in the internal drama most Americans have with the issue of self-abnegation. The Negress serves as a reminder to our sentimental nation that what its countrymen are shaped by is a nonverbal confusion about and, ultimately, abhorrence for the good neighbor policy. Most Americans absorb the principles of the good neighbor policy through the language-based tenets of Judaism and Christianity. These laws lead to a deep emotional confusion about the "good" since most Americans are suspicious of language and spend a great deal of time and energy on Entertainment and Relaxation in an attempt to avoid its net result: Reflection. If the Negress is represented as anything in the media, it is generally as a good neighbor, staunch in her defense of the idea that being a good neighbor makes a difference in this common world. She is also this: a good neighbor uncritical of faith, even as her intellect dissects the byzantine language of the Bible, searching for a truth other than her own. Which is one reason the Negress is both abhorred and adored: for her ability to meld language with belief without becoming sarcastic. Take, for

instance, this story, reported in the *New York Post*: "The
8 Trinidad woman who lost her legs in a subway purse
snatching is not looking for revenge—but she hopes her
mugger becomes 'a better person' in prison. . . . Samela
Thompson, 56, fell onto the tracks in the Van Wyck Boul-
evard station in Jamaica, Queens. . . . She was trying to
jump onto the platform from an E train as she chased a
homeless man who had grabbed her sister's purse. . . . The
feisty mother of five's attitude is 'you have to take life as
it comes.' Thompson wished [her attacker] would know
God."

To women who are not Negresses—some are white—
the Negress, whether she calls herself that or not, is a spec-
ter of dignity—selfless to a fault. But eventually the Negress troubles her noncolored female admirer, since the
latter feels compelled to compare her privilege to what the
Negress does not have—recognizable privilege—and finds
herself lacking. This inversion or competitiveness among
women vis-à-vis their "oppressed" stance says something
about why friendships among women are rare, let alone
why friendships between noncolored women and Negresses are especially so.

For years before and after her death, I referred to myself
as a Negress; it was what I was conditioned to be. And
yet I have come no closer to defining it. In fact, I shy away
from defining it, given my mother's complex reaction to
Negressity for herself and me. I have expressed my Ne-

gressity by living, fully, the prescribed life of an auntie man—what Barbadians call a faggot. Which is a form of kinship, given that my being an auntie man is based on greed for romantic love with men temperamentally not unlike the men my mother knew—that and an unremitting public "niceness." I socialized myself as an auntie man long before I committed my first act as one. I also wore my mother's and sisters' clothes when they were not home; those clothes deflected from the pressure I felt in being different from them. As a child, this difference was too much for me to take; I buried myself in their clothes, their secrets, their desires, to find myself through them. Those women "killed" me, as comedians say when they describe their power over an audience. I wanted them to kill me further by fully exploiting the attention I afforded them. But they couldn't, being women.

Being an auntie man enamored of Negressity is all I have ever known how to be. I do not know what my life would be, or if I *would* be at all, if I were any different.

To say that the public's reaction to my mother's being a Negress and my being one were similar would be egregious. My mother was a woman. Over the years in Brooklyn, she worked as a housekeeper for a relatively well-off Scotsman, as a housekeeper for a Jewish matron, in a beauty salon as a hairdresser, as an assistant in a nursery school. My mother responded to my being a Negress with pride and anger: pride in my identification with women like herself; anger that I identified with her at all. I could not help her react to any of this any differently than she did. This failure haunts me still. I have not catapulted myself past my mother's emotional existence.

Did my mother call herself a Negress as a way of ironically reconciling herself to her history as that most hated of English colonial words, which fixed her as a servant in the eyes of Britain and God? I don't think so, given that she was not especially interested in Britain or history. But "Negress" was one of the few words she took with her when she emigrated from Barbados to Manhattan. As a Negress, her passport to the world was restricted; the world has its limits. Shortly after arriving in New York in the late forties, my mother saw what her everyday life would be; being bright, a high school graduate, and practical, she looked at the world she had emigrated to, picked up her servant's cap, and began starching it with servitude. In her new country, my mother noticed that some New Yorkers retained the fantasy that in writing or speaking about the "underclass," or the "oppressed, silent" woman, or the "indomitable" stoic, they were writing about the kind of Negress she was, but they weren't. My mother was capricious in her views about most things, including race. As a West Indian who lived among other West Indians, my mother did not feel "difference"; she would not allow her feelings to be ghettoized; in her community, she was in the majority. She was capable of giving a nod toward the history of "injustice," but only if it suited her mood.

I think my mother took some pleasure in how harsh the word "Negress" seemed to the citizens in her adopted home. I have perhaps made more of the word "Negress" than my mother meant by it, but I saw and continue to see how it is used to limit and stupidly define the world certain women inhabit. I think my mother took pleasure in manipulating the guilt and embarrassment white and black Americans alike felt when she called herself a Negress, since their view of the Negress was largely sentimental, maudlin, replete with suffering. When my mother laughed in the face of their deeply presumptive view of her, one of her front teeth flashed gold.

My mother disliked the American penchant for euphemism; she was resolute in making the world confront its definition of her. This freed her mind for other things, like her endless illness, which was a protracted form of suicide. From my mother I learned the only way the Negress can own herself is through her protracted suicide; suffering from imminent death keeps people at a distance. I was so lonely knowing her; she was so busy getting to know herself through dying. When my mother became ill with one thing or another, I was eight; by the time my mother died, I was twenty-eight. When she died, I barely knew anything about her at all.

My mother killed herself systematically and not all at once. Perhaps that is because, as a Negress, she had learned stamina, a stamina that consisted of smiling and lying and maintaining the hope that everything would eventually be different, regardless of the facts. Until the end, my mother avoided the facts; she was polite. She would not die. She became ill, and for a long time, which is difficult to cope with; illness silences the well, out of respect. My mother knew that. Being somewhat generous, she acknowledged her children's helplessness in the atmosphere of her dying by allowing us to live with it so that we could see her physical dissolution (clumps of hair, one leg, a few teeth, eventually all gone) without delineating any of its mysteries. Being children, we could only see her imminent death in terms of our imminent loss; we failed to understand what her dying meant to her. She imposed her will by not telling anyone what was really "wrong"; this kept everyone poised and at her service. She would not speak of the facts contributing to her death; nor would she speak of the facts that contributed to her wish to die in the first place. She was quietly spirited, functional, and content in her depression and love; not for the world would she have forfeited the will she applied to disappearing her own body, since it took her so many years to admit to her need for attention, and being ill was one way to get it. The reasons my mother chose to disappear herself, slowly, are manifold. Perhaps she chose to destroy her body out of a profound sadness at the eventual dissolution of her thirty-year romantic relationship with my father; perhaps she chose to disappear her body out of her interest in the discipline inherent in self-abnegation. Perhaps it was both.

My mother first became ill at the end of her love affair with my father. As with most aspects of my parents' relationship, it is unclear whether or not my father dictated the course their relationship would take. The difference between my mother and the woman he became involved with after my mother was significant: she consented to live with my father whereas my mother had not. After my mother refused to marry him, my father never asked her to again. My mother encountered my father's girlfriend once, on the street. My father's new girlfriend was in the company of one of my father's sisters. My mother saw a certain resemblance between my father's new girlfriend and herself: they were both homely but spirited, like Doris Day. It was clear to my mother that his new girlfriend was capable of withstanding my father's tantrums, his compulsive childishness, and his compulsive lying. It was perhaps not as clear to my father's new girlfriend as it was to my mother that my father lied as much as he did because of his need to rebuild the world according to his specifications while being ashamed of this need. Just like a woman.

I think the resemblance my mother saw between herself and my father's new girlfriend shattered any claim to originality my mother had. And, being a woman, she chose to be critical of this similarity rather than judge my father. Shortly afterward, she was made sick by a mysterious respiratory illness. In the end, I think my mother's long and public illness was the only thing she ever felt she experienced as an accomplishment separate from other people. And it was.

When diabetes cost her one of her legs, she said, politely: Oh, I'm dying now. When they removed a gland in her neck as a test for whatever, she said, politely: Oh, I'm really dying now. When one of her kidneys failed completely and a machine functioned in its place, she was still polite. She said: Well, I'm dying. When she lost her vision in one eye, she said she was dying; eventually she could not breathe without stress, and she said she was really dying; her blood pressure was abnormally high, her teeth were bad, she could not urinate or take sugar in her tea or eat pork or remember a conversation, but she remembered these two things: that she was polite and dying.

After they cut off one of her legs for diabetes' sake, she often experienced phantom pain. The world twitched and throbbed. For my mother, experiencing physical pain became a perspective she could own. In pain, she wasn't anything but ill—not a Negress, not a mother of six, not a lover, not a patient. Pain has its own meaning. She passed life by long before she died. When she died, the things she wore in her casket—a wig made of a synthetic fiber colored brown; a white polyester shawl—didn't look as if they belonged to her at all.

MAN SEIZED IN RAPE OF 3 YEAR OLD IN PUBLIC

A Manhattan man raped his 3 year old niece about 25 feet from the F.D.R. Drive at the start of the rush hour Friday evening. . . . The suspect, Leroy Saunders, 29, was caught a few blocks after assaulting the girl under a tree on a grassy knoll. . . . Mr. Saunders, with his pants down to the ankles, assaulted the girl, who was naked below the waist. . . . The girl's mother, who is Mr. Saunders' sister, said, "You just don't expect that from kin." But she declined to talk about the case. "I just want to go back to my apartment to rest," she said. . . . Neighbors said the mother, whose surname differs from her brother's, had six children.

—*The New York Times*, July 17, 1991

That is one story about the Negress. That Leroy Saunders' sister was aged twenty-nine and has a surname different from her brother's are not among the pertinent facts that make up the Negress in her. The fact that his sister did not expect such behavior from "kin" is. This word—"kin"—is a regional colloquialism peculiar to the South; it evokes a narrative. One can imagine Leroy Saunders' sister as an inbred Negress who made her way to New York and bad men and children swollen with need and the welfare system. No husband or father is reported as being attached to her "different" name or to her children. The use of the word "kin" implicated her in Saunders' crime: in a common world, her actions are crimes too. When the Negress is seen in books, such as Toni Morrison's *Beloved* or Terry McMillan's *Waiting to Exhale*, that are marketed according to their "anger" quotient; or in films, such as Charles Burnett's *To Sleep with Anger*, that are remarkable for their willful construction of the "benign" Negress; or in theater pieces, such as *Having Our Say*, that avoid reference to class issues among Negresses; or in newspapers like the one in which I found Leroy Saunders' sister, she is shown as less than herself but is still more than our current cultural climate can handle. Angry or silent, colored and female, her starched cap of servitude firmly in place, she carries a tray loaded with forgiveness, bitterness, rancor, anger, defensiveness, and slatternliness. She has rejected language.

Leroy Saunders' sister's use of the word "kin" indicated not only her commonness to her readers but also her unwillingness to give her brother up, regardless of the facts. The fact is, my mother refused to give me up, despite the Negress in me.

At times my mother disliked the Negress she helped create in me, which is another way she tried to impose her will. (She expressed her will through the phrase "auntie man." When I was five or six years old, my mother and I sat on a bench on a platform in a subway station located near our home. Seated not far off from us was a woman my mother knew from our neighborhood. My mother did not speak to this woman, because she did not like her teenage son, who happened to be with his mother that particular afternoon. Like me, he was a Negress. Unlike me, he dressed the part. He wore black shoes with princess heels, and flesh-colored hose, through which dark hair sprouted, and a lemon-colored shift with grease spots on it, and a purple head scarf, and bangles. He carried a strapless purse, out of which he removed, after little or no consultation with his mother, a compact and lipstick to dress his face too. As my mother looked at that boy, she brushed my eyes closed with the back of her hand. And she hissed the words "auntie man!" I never knew which auntie man she meant.)

The fact that Leroy Saunders' sister, mother of six, three of whom are in foster homes, had to "rest" after her daughter's attack on a grassy knoll and perhaps consider the facts later was not an unusual characteristic, given what I assumed when I read her story: that she was a Negress. What was or perhaps was not unusual, given that there was no photograph accompanying "Man Seized in Rape of 3 Year Old," was that immediately upon reading it, I attached black faces to this narrative of "kin" gone awry, a grassy knoll, pants down around the ankles, and a mother's need for "rest" after an atrocity committed against someone else.

The story of the Negress is not difficult to understand if you listen. My sisters spoke the same language of kin for kin, one saying of another: "She is so nasty. Having one baby after another, and none of them by the same father. Like a dog." Any story resembling this one I assumed I owned, in the way that I assumed Leroy Saunders' sister was "mine," being another Negress living in strict avoidance of the facts, just as I assumed his niece was "mine," being another Negress left to a world where her future actions will probably illustrate Leroy Saunders' turn of mind against her. What the *Times* made clear was how Leroy Saunders' sister and niece would not be a story were it not for him.

Perhaps the man I fucked when I was ten wanted to have the same effect on me that Leroy Saunders had on his sister, niece, or readers. I do not remember him very well, but it was partially through him that I came into my inheritance as a Negress. He worked as a janitor in the apartment building where one of my sisters lived. He was black. He was wearing blue cotton trousers and a blue cotton shirt. He pushed his trousers down around his ankles. He said: You're pretty. He said: Sit on this, and I did. He held me. He thought I was frightened but I wasn't. I performed vulnerability in the hope that it would elicit his maleness. He does not know that I exist still, nor that I grew up forever in the moment I seduced him into taking that nasty turn with me. For years, I thought all of this was a dream, but it wasn't. Seducing men into performing acts defined as male, but in circumstances they would describe as illicit (two scenarios men consider illicit: they have a girlfriend or live with someone else), disempowers their maleness. In an illicit circumstance, men are just as frightened and vulnerable as the next guy. That's what I like. This desire can be developed in childhood and follow you into adulthood, or whatever. That's what your life becomes; it's governed by emotional patterns that distort your reason, or become your reason.

For years I could not face my own complicity with the man in the blue cotton shirt and blue cotton pants. I could not face the way in which I had wanted him to make me a Negress, or the fact that I wanted to be consumed by him so that I could be part of a narrative as compelling to me as my mother's was, a narrative in which I too would be involved with a bad man, resulting in heartache that would eventually lead to depression, an endless suicide, and the attention that can be garnered from all that.

I was dwarfed by my mother's spectacular sense of narrative and disaster; she could have been a great writer. I have never been comforted by the idea that writing her narrative down, in fragments, is at all equal to the power of her live-while-trying-not-to experience. She is so interesting to me—as a kind of living literature. I still envy her allure. And I still envy her ability to love—no matter how terrible, no matter how coarse—and to allow that love to consume her, or, literally, parts of herself. I stand back from the model of her courage, just as I stand back from my desire to be taken in by love, even as I fear its power. I avoid all of this even though I have considered myself a Negress in the tradition of my mother. But I tremble at the thought of losing a leg, and having the world twitch before me because of love. In general, I avoid my mother's remarkable way of being. She had six children whom she cared for, more often than not lovingly, though she remained unconvinced that having children was the solution to the issue of isolation. She did not regard isolation as a problem but something else to think about, whereas I have never been able to view it as anything but the result of separation. Time has not changed my point of view, nor has the knowledge that what divide people are not the dreary marginal issues of race, or class, or gender, but this: those who believe friendship and love dispel our basic aloneness, and those who do not. This was the difference that divided me from my mother. Maybe all I can say in support of my difference from her is that she never missed herself while I was around.

My mother's long, slow, public death was an advertisement for the life she had lived—good or bad is not the point. And not having much control over my thoughts regarding Negressity is beside the point too. What continues to interest me is why my mother, like most women, could never decide which she preferred: to live and to grow, or to die while retaining bitterness and hope.

Having grown up surrounded by the story of the Negress, which has no primary text, I can only piece together a narrative about my mother based on the facts. Certain facts about my mother's religious, cultural, culinary, sexual, sartorial, and humanitarian interests: She attended Sunday services at St. George's Episcopal Church, a Gothic structure in the Bedford-Stuyvesant section of Brooklyn, surrounded by brownstones, vacant lots, and children. My mother had attended services at St. George's ever since she emigrated to New York as a young girl of seventeen. The congregation was largely West Indian and judgmental of my mother because she had chosen not to marry my father while choosing to have his children. Many of the women in that congregation had children out of wedlock as well, but they judged my mother just the same, because she wasn't bitter about not being married. At St. George's, my mother sometimes sang, in her sweet, reedy voice, "I Surrender All," her favorite hymn.

She also loved the foods of her country: sous, blood pudding, coconut bread, coo-coo. She enjoyed her own mother most when her mother prepared those foods for her on certain holidays: birthdays, Christmas, wakes.

She herself was a mediocre cook who tried to be better at it than she was by preparing elaborate meals culled from French cookbooks. I learned to cook in reaction to the meals my mother prepared. She had no idea what food might be pleasing to other people since she spent much of her time in her own head and body.

She was very clear about being her own person. She never said, "I didn't mean to," or "I couldn't help it," or "I'm sorry." She rarely changed her mind except to accommodate someone else's change of mind. When she lied, it was to spare someone else the embarrassment of feeling too much.

She didn't change her surname after she left her first and only husband. All of her children had the same last name, even though my father's last name is Williams. She didn't notice her children's embarrassment when they addressed my father as "Mr. Als" and he corrected them.

She loved the ocean. She didn't return to Barbados until shortly before she died, but the Caribbean Sea was the subject of her conversation from time to time. Summers, my brother and I were sent to Barbados with packages of clothes and food as gifts. From time to time, the girl children of cousins and aunts she hadn't seen for years came to stay with us. My brother and I didn't like Barbados, but we loved our mother, and preferred to imagine the island through her memories of it. In 1978, when I was seventeen, I read a story by a writer from the West Indies. The story, "Wingless," had been written by Jamaica Kincaid. In it, I read this description of the Caribbean Sea and its surroundings: "The sea, the shimmering pink-colored sand, the swimmers with hats, two people walking arm in arm, talking in each other's face, dots of water landing on noses, the sea spray on ankles, on overdeveloped calves, the blue, the green, the black, so deep, so smooth, a great and swift undercurrent, glassy, the white wavelets." This story changed everything. It taught me how language could be made visual and how memory combined with the imagination made the visual resonate. After reading this story, I read it aloud to my mother, as she sat before me, dying. After I read it, my mother said: "Exactly."

She loved the ocean. My father was loving toward my mother and his children when he took us to the ocean. Even after he had lived with his new girlfriend for quite some time, he still took us to see the waves, the sand, people. I watched my parents' adult feet become tiny in the huge expanse of sand.

She was in love with my father until the end. They spoke every day on the telephone. They amused and angered one another. She called him "Cyp," which was short for Cyprian, his given name. When he said her name, Marie, he said it in a thick Bajun accent, so that the "a" was very flat. In his mouth, her name sounded like this: "Mare-ee."

She ignored my father when he broadcast his news of the world. She knew that his recounting of certain newspaper facts—murders, boroughs blasted by crime and poverty—was really just my father going over the ground of his paranoia and infantile hysteria again. Until I was old enough to realize all of that for myself, I believed my father; after a while I didn't. Now I have a desultory interest in fact, and a profound interest in what the imagination can do.

She lived, for many years, with my younger brother, my older sister (eleven years my senior and the one closest to me in age), and me, in a two-story brownstone in the Flatbush section of Brooklyn. The house had a narrow staircase. We lived in the apartment above the elderly Jewish couple who owned the building, Mr. and Mrs. Schwartz. Sometimes my brother and I would watch television with the Schwartzes. I marveled at the orderliness of Mr. and Mrs. Schwartz's home, the strange smells, the candles that they burned on Friday nights. I was ten when we went to live with the Schwartzes. I loved them. I wanted to be a Jew. I told Mrs. Schwartz: I want to be a Jew, but how? One day, when I was with my mother, Mrs. Schwartz stopped my mother on that narrow staircase to tell her that I wanted to be a Jew. I was ten. My mother looked at me. She told Mrs. Schwartz that I wanted to be a *writer*. Shortly afterward, Mrs. Schwartz gave me a gift. It was a typewriter that had belonged to her son, The *Doctor*.

She told one story about being a servant among the Jews when she was a young girl new to America. She lived in Brooklyn. With other teenage girls her age, she would go to the Flatbush section and wait on a particular street corner for people—mostly Jews—to drive by in their big cars, from which they would look to see which girls on that street corner were healthy and clean enough to do day work in their homes. "We called ourselves Daily Woikers," my mother said, in a Yiddish-American accent, laughing.

She called me "Bubala" from time to time in a strong Yiddish-American accent.

She took me with her to Delancey Street, on the Lower

East Side, in Manhattan, to go shopping from time to
time. Many Jews owned stores there. She was comfortable
with what she called "The Jews."

She had been denied many things because of her attraction to men like her father, who had denied her everything. He was the only person I ever heard her complain
about. Having been denied many things, she denied her
children next to nothing.

She didn't know that when she began being ill and my
older sister, brother, and I were forced to stay with our
father's mother for a while, that we went to the Apollo
Theatre in Harlem against our grandmother's wishes to
see James Brown—she thought he was a "bad American"—whose records we loved and listened to at Birdel's
Record Shop on Nostrand Avenue, in the Bedford-
Stuyvesant section of Brooklyn, because we couldn't af-
ford to buy them, nor could we listen to them in our
grandmother's home. We went to the Apollo to see James
Brown in the late sixties, when he still marcelled his hair.
We saved money for the tickets by selling glass soda bottles back to the grocer. James Brown was a marvel in his
blue silk suit and pointy shoes. He performed being "over-
whelmed" by his own musicianship—the first viable aesthetic I ever saw. Onstage, his hair and clothes were as
perfect as any Negress's I had ever seen.

She was not ambitious for her children, but she was
supportive of their ambitions. When I was eight I told her
I wanted to be a writer. Writing things down was the only
way I understood how to be heard, there being so many
women in my mother's house at various times, talking.

For years after I told my mother I wanted to be a writer, she would give me, as Christmas presents, writing tablets to write things down in; she would also give me books to read that she brought from the Liberation Bookshop on Nostrand Avenue. The books were almost always books of poems or novels, and were almost always by women, such as Alice Childress' *A Hero Ain't Nothin' but a Sandwich, Maud Martha*, by Gwendolyn Brooks, and anything by Paule Marshall. In between reading all of that, I also read *A Tree Grows in Brooklyn*, by Betty Smith, more than once.

She spent many hours with me alone, in the dark, in her bedroom, listening to me lie. Somehow she knew that most writers became writers after having spent their childhood lying. Or perhaps she didn't know that at all. She was extremely tolerant of my lies. She was interested in where my lies could take her.

She was not impatient with my pretensions. When, at thirteen or fourteen, I began wearing a silk ascot to school and took to writing by the light of a kerosene lamp like my hero at the time, Horace Greeley, the famous nineteenth-century journalist, she didn't say a word.

She read Truman Capote when I discovered him. I was twelve. She liked *Other Voices, Other Rooms*, but didn't discuss it with me. I read that novel over and over again, fascinated by its oblique homosexual "theme" and, even more so, by the photograph of Truman Capote on the back of the book, lying on a sofa, looking like a homely but spirited young girl waiting to be admired by someone like my father. After we read *Breakfast at Tiffany's* she took me to Tiffany's. We couldn't eat there, so we went to Schrafft's wearing our beige trench coats in the rain.

She became a hairdresser in a beauty salon when I was five; she was a hairdresser by profession until I was twelve or so. She called the salon "the shop." It was frequented by Negresses. I went there after school. At the shop, my mother wore a white smock. She straightened hair and rubbed bergamot into women's scalps. She listened to women talk all day. After a while, problems became pretty general to her. People complained, no matter what; she learned that for some people complaining was a way of being. After a while, she didn't respond to her customers' problems; she knew they didn't want a solution. I heard my mother's customers speak of their problems too, but I reacted emotionally. My mother knew better. She heard women complain about their husbands who blah, blah, blah; their children who blah, blah, blah. The more she heard, the more general my mother became in her support and encouragement of everyone. She addressed most of those women as "Honey" because after a while she couldn't remember their names.

She loved *Crime and Punishment*. She read it over and over again while locked in the bathroom, her only refuge before she began dying. Her second favorite novel was Paule Marshall's *Brown Girl, Brownstones*, the story of a Brooklyn-based girl named Selina who is of Bajun descent. Selina wears gold bangles; the bangles are part of her sartorial heritage, the myth being that you can always sell the bangles to book passage back to Barbados. Selina does not take that myth to heart. At the end of the novel, Selina throws her bangles in a pile of rubbish in an empty lot in Brooklyn. My mother passed this book on to me. I read it eleven times. I was eleven years old. I read the author's biography on the jacket flap, and looked up her name in the Manhattan telephone directory. When Paule Marshall answered the telephone, I told her, in a rush, about how much my mother loved her novel and how we did not live very far from where Selina had grown up. Paule Marshall was amazed. She made her son pick up the extension and listen in. Later, when I told my mother what I had done, she looked at me in amazement. She knew that I had telephoned Paule Marshall for both of us because I considered my mother's rarely ventured opinion important.

She had a mind similar to mine, which is to say a mind that is attracted to self-expression as it is filtered through an elliptical thought process—writers that don't tell the full story, movies that don't have much exposition, and so on. We weren't alike emotionally; in the end, I am a moralist and she was not. I think all that was interesting to both of us, but I can't speak for her.

She took adult education classes for a year, five or six years before her leg was cut off. She had to read Sophocles' Oedipus plays. She had trouble grasping the conflict.

She was very visual and had a quiet, minimal style of dress. She didn't read fashion magazines, pay attention to trends, or have enough money to be fashionable. Each of her daughters made many of their own clothes, or she made clothes for them. Many people remarked on her daughters' unique style, which was an amalgamation of some aspects of West Indian style (gold bangles, gold earrings, loafers), American style (circle skirts or straight skirts with kick pleats and silk backing; cardigans), and their individual style (orange lipstick and, eventually, nose rings).

She had one fox-fur stole, a gold front tooth, short, loosely curled hair, small feet that had been misshapen from many years of wearing shoes that were two sizes too small. When they cut off one of her legs, my eldest sister said to our mother, "Well, at least we won't have to look at those two ugly feet anymore." My mother laughed.

She loved to dance. When she was a young girl, friends used to call her the Girl of a Thousand Steps. My father did not like to dance. Perhaps they learned a great deal about other people through knowing one another.

She had performed the role of Buttercup in *H.M.S. Pinafore* when she was a schoolgirl. Sometimes, in the morning, when she was opening the drapes and I would groan at the encroaching sunlight, she would sing, "I'm called little Buttercup / Poor little Buttercup / Though I could never tell why." Without prompting, she would also sometimes sing Joyce Kilmer's "Trees."

She dropped her West Indian accent a few years after she became a U.S. citizen in the late forties. She didn't like people who capitalized on being exotic. She didn't like accents in general. She lived in America and wanted to sound like an American. She did, unless she was angry. She thought accents were rude in America, especially if the accent was British. Having a British accent after living in America for a time was, to her, like mourning one's privileged relationship to a disappointed and disappointing empire, or imposing one's privilege on a new land. She moved on when she could. She was not nostalgic but she cherished everyone else's past.

She had one friend who was an auntie man. Unlike other women who knew him as well, my mother didn't find her friend's sexual predilection confusing or anger-provoking. Besides, auntie men were not mysterious beings to her; in Barbados, most ostensibly straight men had sex with them, which was good, since that left women alone for a while. During the course of her friendship with Grantly the auntie man, she focused on him. Had she had access to other people besides her children, lover, employer, doctors, she might have been a fag hag, fond of auntie men, music, and movies.

She loved Mary Astor in the film version of *The Maltese Falcon*. In that movie Mary Astor is undone by her deceit. She also loved Mary Astor's short haircut and little gold hoop-shaped earrings. At one point, when I told my mother that the playwright George S. Kaufman, who was married, had given Mary Astor those earrings at the height of their "illicit" affair, she laughed.

She had a romantic attachment to Kim Novak in the film version of *Picnic*. In it, Kim Novak describes herself as a pretty girl "who gets tired of being looked at." In particular, my mother liked the rendition of "Moonglow" that plays in the film, to which Kim Novak, wearing a blue dress, dances with William Holden. They do not speak while they dance; they fall in love without talking.

She was intrigued by the sexually repressed atmosphere in Elia Kazan's film *Splendor in the Grass*. She disliked sexually explicit language. She was a product of her time in this respect only.

She knew of one entertainer. She was friends with a man who worked as a gardener for the Pleshette family in Westchester. The Pleshettes had a daughter, Suzanne, who was an actress best known for her work as Bob Newhart's wife on *The Bob Newhart Show*.

She also loved Merle Oberon in *Wuthering Heights*. One scene from that film haunted us. The antiheroine, Cathy, is in the kitchen with Ellen discussing her childhood love, Heathcliff, whom she'd like to abolish from her life, but can't. A flash of thunder illuminates Cathy's soft and greedy face when she says, "Ellen, I *am* Heathcliff." Cathy's identification with Heathcliff is the dramatic center of the film; my propensity for identifying with women has been the dramatic center of my life. My mother was spirited but not imaginative.

She didn't like Eartha Kitt or Billie Holiday. She considered Eartha Kitt pretentious. When I was twenty, I began playing Billie Holiday records all the time; I was interested in how disaffection could be conveyed in a narrative structure. My mother said: "Why do you play those albums all the time? When I saw Billie Holiday perform, she looked quite respectable."

She had a real sense of most things. She could not bear how interracial children with red or blond hair looked. She called them "riny," meaning they reminded her of orange rind. She did not have much resistance to the idea of any of her children being involved with an American white person, or a European, since she associated white people with ghosts. In her culture, ghosts were called "dupies" and could be useful: they frightened one's enemies away, or came to one in dreams and unraveled mysteries the troubled dreamer found disturbing. She used to say that if any one of her children became involved with a dupie, the least they could be was attractive. She did not like to see white people dance.

She could not bear the false idea of happy families. To her, children who had grown up in a happy family inherited a tragic hope: that they could replicate their memory of familial unity in their own homes. But they never learned how, resisting any experience other than the categorically "wonderful." She saw those children remain children as they complained about a world their parents never made, which, in turn, they could never inhabit.

She never used the sanctimonious tone of voice most women she knew used when they discussed their children; she disliked the morally "correct" attitude most women she knew adopted after giving birth, dividing the world into those women who were "good" because they had children and those women who were morally disreputable because they didn't. She saw the issue of children as just one more opportunity for women to be competitive among themselves. Two reasons she had children were, one: an opportunity to experience unconditional love, and, two: her curiosity about how lives get lived. With a child, who knew what would happen next?

She was slightly ambivalent about my appearance. Even when I was no longer a small boy, I was Cute and Adorable in a way reminiscent of illustrations of generic Negro boys on Hallmark cards. Sometimes she preferred my brother's company to mine. He was quieter and less emotional. I always wanted something from her.

She didn't like it when her sons began experimenting

with certain aspects of boyishness, like spitting on sidewalks or jamming their fists in the pockets of their jeans. She couldn't imagine what most boys meant by anything.

She invited homeless women into her home for the afternoon, where she offered them a cup of tea and unmitigated attention. They were women whom she came across in our neighborhood. When she saw them, she would stop and invite them up. I do not think my mother identified with the women she brought in, but I did. I felt my desire to be a Negress looked as mad as their misfortune. I feared my desire to be like my mother and sister looked as disjunctive to the women in my family as those homeless women looked to me, with their long, filthy scarves draped across the clear, crunchy plastic covering my mother's pink velour sofa, their giant oil-stained shopping bags filled with (I imagined) junk, money, and diaries, all of which crackled at their homeless feet, the same feet that burned holes in the roses patterning my mother's dusty polyester living-room rug.

That I was a Negress became clear to me when I was thirteen. My mother's leg had yet to be cut off, but she already had diabetes. That year, I went to a party being held by one of my mother's relatives. I didn't know why my mother had not attended the party until I returned home and told her about it. We were standing in the kitchen. I told her how I had met a man there who had asked after her. I described him: bald head, a square figure, very dark skin. I met him on the stoop leading away from the house where the party was being held. I remembered everything about the meeting and spoke of it excitedly. I didn't tell my mother about the man's charm and my attraction to his charm. Nor did I describe the roundness of the orange sun setting behind his large brown head; rubbing my moist hands against the stoop's bumpy concrete; admiring his graceful saunter as he walked away. My mother's face became hard when I mentioned his first name, Eldred. She would not look at me as she said: "That was the man I was married to. That was my husband." The air was still between us; it became a wall. I knew I was a Negress because of the jealousy I felt over her having left someone I coveted. I glanced at my mother; her face, her body told me that she had been where I wanted to be long before I began imagining being a Negress. We stood in the kitchen for quite some time. I saw myself in my mother's eyes; the reflection showed a teenage girl, insecure, frightened, and vengeful.

As a pubescent Negress, I spent a great deal of time in thrall to the sister who was closest to me in age and who continued to live at home for years after our older sisters had left.

She created a world in her bedroom that resonated with spitefulness and intellectual possibility. In her room, we danced to Dionne Warwick singing "Don't Make Me Over" as she began getting dressed for the evening. She was the only college student I knew. From her asking my advice on what to wear, I knew she was pleased that I was absorbed by being a Negress. My empathy for her bordered on repression: in order to be like her, I couldn't admit to having a self that was in the least different. Sometimes, in a sudden fit of pique, she would demand to know what I was anyway, hanging around a girl's bedroom. In those moments, I was startled into accepting our difference: she was competitive with me; she felt my Negressity would eventually loom over hers. I was tall, and already better at Negressity then she was.

She was beautiful. She had long legs and a long neck and a keen intelligence. She had black shoulder-length hair that she wore in a chignon. She also wore straight skirts and cardigans and flats. She was adored by many men; she was not ambivalent about their adoration. "Who says people don't love objects?" she asked me once. She had many lovers, which prompted one sister to say about her later, "She's so nasty. . . . Like a dog." Her physicality and sartorial sense was a style—my first brush with that powerful conundrum. Through her, I became fascinated by the question of appearance, and how it manifested itself in the popular music of the girl groups we listened to as my sister got dressed for the evening. Their music was lyrical; those girl groups had names like clothing: the Shirelles, the Chiffons, the Ronettes. The records had been left behind in our mother's apartment by our older sisters. Those girl groups were armies of female perfection. Through them, we began to understand the continued popularity of black dance music, and two concepts it expressed, which my sister and I knew were not conjoined: "reality" and "fantasy." We understood how the Crystals' "He Hit Me (and It Felt Like a Kiss)" introduced the painful exigencies of Negressity to popular music. We understood how "Dancin' in the Streets" by Martha and the Vandellas advocated funk as the ultimate fantasy or "trip," serving as a release for Negresses made to feel common in this common world.

My sister's style became more complicated as she grew older and began to admire other aspects of American culture. When she was in her early twenties, her makeup and dress became the physical realization of the music she loved most: jazz. She applied large amounts of rouge to her cheeks and forehead; she wore white lipstick. She had one hairdo that looked like an open book standing on its spine. The more my sister became interested in certain facets of American culture, the more her body resembled a sound without a scale. My mother made some perfunctory objections to my sister's extreme makeup, but silently she admired her because you couldn't not admire her if you were in the least visual. My sister played the trumpet and wore my father's mother's old clothes and kept her hair up in one interesting design or another, but she never moved past the parameters of her bedroom wall into the world with any of this. Through her, I learned what the moral impulse behind making art was: doing it for yourself because it expressed bits of this, bits of that, all making up a person. She had a fascinating inability to separate her mind from her body or either from music. She was a great writer who could only perform it.

Her other interests included reading Milton, and Spenser's *The Faerie Queene*. She would lock herself in the bathroom, where she wrote poetry in a strange hand; on the page, she wrote her poems sideways instead of up and down. In the bathroom, she also wrapped her sanitary napkins in newspapers and shoved them in the pipe that stood between the toilet seat and a crumbling wall. She never explained why she did this, and no one asked her why, just as no one asked me why I sometimes wore her drawers.

I learned a little about Negressity from her as I sat crouched behind her bedroom door, listening to her experience some of the words she could not join together to tell her story. Perhaps she didn't want to tell her story, but I wanted her to. Lying first with one man and then another, like a dog, she would say, over and over again, "Oh, oh, oh." Perhaps my sister's word was uttered in disappointment; I'm not sure. Listening to her word, I wanted to hear disappointment since I was disappointed that I was not physically a woman. Hearing disappointment, I immediately formed a narrative inside my head: that men provoked the experience of words; that the words the Negress utters during her experience with one man or another are about her disappointment. When I was with the man in the blue khaki trousers and blue khaki shirt, I didn't utter a word, having already memoized my sister's.

I grew up with my sister during the seventies, a period characterized by a breakdown in the traditional social order, at least as we had known it. We didn't pay much attention to our "times."

The seventies were a synthetic version of the more successful active radicalism of the sixties. As a leftover time, the seventies suited our Negressity perfectly since we considered ourselves leftover people. Although we did not know it then, my sister and I used our cursory involvement in the Black Power movement—sit-ins in Harlem, many, many poetry readings in the Bronx, and demonstrations everywhere—to catapult ourselves past our mother's increasing disinterest in the world at large. Being younger and, in some respects, less intelligent than our mother, we were conscious of wanting to develop our own social stance, even as we affected hers, because we admired her. I think we misread our mother's exhausted concern as lack of concern; she never didn't care. Unlike our mother, we affected an interest in people who, because they had the same skin color as our own, presumed we were interested in the race and its struggle. We were not interested in the race and its struggle. We were not interested in strident abstractions, being so emotionally abstract ourselves. We were West Indians living in New York; we were smug in our sense of displacement; we took freely from both cultures in order to be unselfconsciously interesting. The furor and energy that our black American contemporaries focused on dreams and hopes, we found ridiculous. Their ideology was totalitarianism made simple: economic independence from "the man," an entirely black-run government, and so on. We were especially amused by the movement's xenophobia. Xenophobes first, members of the Black Power movement referred to West Indians, and their ambitious progeny, as black Jews.

Being our mother's children, we had no interest in the world at large, especially if its events did not reflect our individual internal worlds.

We adopted the revolution as our cause; it was a chance to brush up against a reality that was distant enough from our mother and her imminent death. By 1975, when I was fourteen, my sister and I had not been aware of much outside our mother's by then six-year-old suffering. Marching in Harlem for a separate-but-equal economic system, or watching my sister bed one or two or five black revolutionaries who still lived at home with their respective moms and who used their nationalist rhetoric and nonthink speak in a vain attempt to impersonate the kind of man my sister and her ilk imagined they wanted, was, for me, oddly preferable to our mother's voice saying: Well, I'm dying.

It is not outrageous of me to say that my sister and I probably considered American blacks disgusting on some level, even though we didn't admit this to ourselves, given our melodramatic silence and "feelings." We weren't attracted to much that we didn't find repugnant. I believe we probably thought American blacks were awful because they weren't us. We wanted to save them from themselves. We were very big on rescuing people, having had a mother. On the other hand, we hated our older sisters' smug Negress disapproval of anything that wasn't them, even as we tried to imitate them by not liking white people—for a while.

My sister discovered Black Power around the same time

she discovered her need for a father; the movement was the inversion of our father's cruel teasing; as a concept it lent itself to the fantasy of "serious" black men who were "committed." My sister was drawn to Black Power because of its distinctly American male cast of mind. As a girl of West Indian descent, she considered American black men exotic, charming in their narcissism and in their ahistorical stance and desultory desire for social change.

The part of our outings I looked forward to most was not picketing or canvassing votes for now forgotten community leaders, but listening to women who sometimes took the stands at rallies and spoke, women who wrote and published books and recited their words in public, unlike my sister, who hid or burned her diary, and buried her language in the creases of her careless lovers' necks.

The women writers we heard recite their verse—Sonia Sanchez and Nikki Giovanni—were addressed as Sister. They wore brightly colored dashikis and robes. Their poetic skills were limited. Their work was strident, empty, and invigorating. They valorized the black male. In actual fact, the black male those poetesses and my sister imagined did not exist, which is one reason they had to imagine him. Those women embraced the ideology spouted during the revolution that was always about to be, because they wanted to maintain the fantasy that the revolution was the assertion of a black masculinity that was about to happen. That masculinity would serve my sister's purpose: it would be forceful enough to dismantle Negressity and its aura of depression. That the male fraction of the black revolutionary movement was irresponsible and childlike was also beside the point. The fact that the male fraction of the black revolutionary movement was in search of the same authority figure—Dad—that their female comrades were looking for was beside the point. What made the women different from the men in the movement was interesting: the will those women applied to creating Dad, which their black male counterparts couldn't.

The poetesses my sister and I heard wrote verse that was essentially romantic, devoid of fact or observation, an outgrowth of early "imperialist" influences, like *Jane Eyre*. In the delusional fervor of a revolution that did not take place, the poetesses we heard and read imagined, like my sister, that the black male was poised on the brink of becoming what they wanted him to be: invincible, domineering, revolutionary. But "maleness" is not a viable construct in colored life. Colored life is matriarchal; any matriarchal society can be defined as colored.

If maleness manages to brush up against the Negress, it is usually violent, so its presence is felt. And it eventually absents itself from the Negress because the Negress's intellectual and physical focus on surviving diminishes any and all ideas maleness has about being central; there's no room for it. The Negress's will to survive is enhanced by her need to survive for her children. But being the source of such strength is sometimes too much for the Negress. Sometimes she contrives to marry something other than herself or her children in order to escape it, that something being the product of her indefatigable will, an invention: a black male. My sister eventually married one after the revolution; she rebelled against my mother's brand of independence by marrying not for love but to prove a point: that she could be dominated by her invention—a black male. Her marriage didn't last long. Even disguised as a wife, my sister had a hard time masking her intelligence.

The poetesses my sister and I listened to commanded the respect of their male "comrades" because they were inventing them as officers of war. As those women poets spoke in their conspiratorial, syncopated voices, another tone expressive of something other than the self-congratulatory broke in. That tone expressed their need for Daddy to shut them up. As those women poets spoke, it became clear to me that their language was not the product of reflection or the desire to reflect; if they thought before they spoke, they'd be forced to realize that what they were screaming about was their need to be silenced. Instead, they called their need to be oppressed by the black male who does not exist an emergent black tradition, its foundation being abstractions: Black Motherhood and Black Pride.

The movement's most popular poet, Nikki Giovanni, wrote in a poem titled "Seduction," published in 1970:

one day
you gonna walk in this house
and i'm gonna have on a long African
gown
you'll sit down and say "The Black . . ."
and i'm gonna take one arm out
then you—not noticing me at all—will say "What about
this brother . . ."
and i'm going to be slipping it over my head
and you'll rapp on about "The revolution . . ."
while i rest your hand against my stomach
you'll go on—as you always do—saying

"i just can't dig . . ."

while i'm moving your hand up and down
and i'll be taking your dashiki off . . .
then you'll notice
your state of undress
and knowing you you'll just say
"Nikki,
isn't this counterrevolutionary . . . ?"

And Sonia Sanchez wrote in "Black Magic": "magic /
my man / is you / turning / my body into / a thousand
smiles. / black magic is your / touch / making / me
breathe."

In each of these poems, the Negress does not take responsibility for herself, let alone another Negress. Nor
does intimacy exist between her and anyone remotely
identifiable as a person. Rather, these poems, and the
many others like them, are evidence of the mind's ability
to convince itself that it has talent; before these poetesses
displayed themselves on the page, they had the approval
of an audience.

During the revolution, the Negress replaced her
starched cap of servitude with a brightly colored turban
made of kinte cloth, but she did not reinvent her internal
structure. And like much of the work written by and
about the Negress during that period, the images they offered in their verse—a simple, uncomplicated, thuggish
sexuality projected onto that phantom construction, the
black male—was perfectly legitimate but dumb, easily co-
optable by the pornographic imagination that continues
to produce magazines such as *Black Tail, Sugah,* and *Eb-*

ony Heat, in the uncontested knowledge that the Negress is nothing if not accommodating to her audience.

Despite the revolution's collapse into other black ideologies, which have all been based on a longing for a daddy who could destroy colored matriarchy, my sister continued to believe a revolution would come. But not really. She was in thrall to her criticism of the revolution's poetesses: "They're bad writers and ineffectual as leaders," she said. This freed my sister from the guilt she felt about not liking other Negresses very much at all.

After the revolution, my sister became interested in astrology and "primitive" painting. She rejected the idea of language being transformative of anything. She became a Muslim for a while, among other things. She moved to Kansas with her husband, who was a Muslim. They moved to get away from Brooklyn. She wrote to me that she loved the men in Kansas, with their big Stetsons and pointy boots; she loved any part of the world that had a strong aesthetic, or an aesthetic that she could identify as indigenous to the place she was in. She had children. She had learned certain things about motherhood from our mother, but being more theatrically intelligent and spiteful than our mother, she rarely made room for her children to exercise their own intelligence. My sister refused to suffer much of anything, let alone because she was a Negress.

. . .

My sister's disappointment in being a Negress was nearly equal to my interest in Negresses like my sister. As I grew up, it became increasingly clear that one of the reasons behind my sister's occasional sharp annoyance with me was this: she wanted me to be a black male and give up being a Negress so that she could see herself in contrast to me, rather than as a competitor. As I grew older, it became clear that my mother and other sisters wanted me to become a black male for the same reasons. I thought being an auntie man was a fair compromise, but it wasn't enough. They wanted me to be in the world as a black man who was for *and* against them. Ultimately, the weight of my being a Negress was too much. For a time, I tried to give it up, because I adored them. I went out into the world. I became a student and, eventually, an office worker. I was too emotional to do either very well. I failed to recognize the students and workers I was supposed to compete with, because I was intent on being a good neighbor. It is difficult to be Negress-identified, since the Negress rarely identifies with herself.

That the Negress exists somewhere between her "good" public image and "bad" pornographic one accounts for her continued popularity. One popular story about the Negress appears in a very bad American novel titled *Imitation of Life*, published in 1932 by Fannie Hurst (Douglas Sirk adapted this novel for the screen in 1959). Annie the Negress gives birth to a girl, Sarah Jane, who blames the absence of her "practically white" father on her very black, very forgiving mother. Sarah Jane grows to hate her mother's propensity to forgive. Annie the Negress casts a pall over her daughter's speech; she punishes her daughter for wanting to separate from her by being tyrannically nice—a niceness that Sarah Jane cleaves to and despises but never frees herself from. Annie the Negress continues to live on in popular novels being written by American blacks today. In most of the books written by Gayl Jones, Toni Cade Bambara, Toni Morrison, John Edgar Wideman, and Terry McMillan, the author becomes Sarah Jane in relation to the Negresses they create; they never question what the Negress means, because they cannot face her; if they do, it is as a symbol of the physical distance they would like to put between themselves and the Negress's ability to overwhelm her progeny—or her recorders. In their books, the Negress is shut off from ideas or speech of her own as she dons the cap of servitude, incapable of explaining what goes on beneath it. Like the mother in Toni Cade Bambara's *Gorilla, My Love*:

It does no good to write autobiographical fiction cause the minute the book hits the stand here comes your mama screamin how could you and sighin death where is they sting and she snatches you up out your bed to grill you about what was going down back there in Brooklyn when she was working three jobs and trying to improve the quality of your life and come to find . . . that you were messin around with that nasty boy up the block and breaks into sobs.

Or like Eva, another mother, in Gayl Jones's *Eva's*

Man:

He undressed me and he was sweating. And then he held onto my shoulders and drew me toward him and I was naked and sweating, not with my own sweat, but with his sweat. He had no tenderness, no none, and then he laid me on my back on the bed. He didn't play first. No, he went in before I was ready. . . .

"Felt good, didn't it?"

"Yes."

"I bet it felt good."

"Yes."

"You could've shared it with me."

"What am I doing?"

"You fucking me."

"What am I doing?"

"You fucking me."

In describing the Negress, writers describe themselves away from her as they rush headlong into the void of patriarchy. In their books, the Negress is replete with tears. She smiles. Her chest heaves. Her body is that of a servant not begging for respite. She burns brightly in the imagination, like a dull witch. In order to understand her, I have written my life in the margins of hers. Is this love? How did I love my mother? After a certain point, I rarely expressed it physically for fear her touch would be so hideous and lonely. How do I love her still? In my imagination.

.   .   .

What would the Negress be if she were stripped of her role? Would she be just another banal woman undone by domestic despair, held upright by her class aspirations and fantasies about being fulfilled through marriage? Given the written material in which she appears, it is difficult to feel one is in the presence of a person; by extension, it is difficult to imagine her making an appearance in literature as anything other than a tiresome colored woman, weeping over her attempts to be a good neighbor. It is difficult to imagine the Negress being anything other than what she has come to symbolize in contemporary literature: authorial conceit. What Bambara, Jones et al. are at pains to disguise is that the Negress represents their ambition: they are intent on building an empirical universe in which the only voices heard are their own, and since the Negress does not speak, but *moves* through their fiction as either an adventurer or a victim, she is dependent upon the fictional system they build for her in order to exist at all. Part of that system is based on this dialectic: creating the Negress in order to kill her since she represents the matriarchal society these authors are at pains to forget, even as they cling to the Negress because of her ability to milk sympathy from the audience—or provide it.

In most contemporary fiction, the Negress is rarely allowed to express authority, let alone be responsible for another woman, as Grace Strasser-Mendana is in Joan Didion's novel *A Book of Common Prayer*: "I will be her witness. That would translate *seré su testigo*, and will not appear in your traveler's phrasebook because it is not a useful phrase for the prudent traveler." Nor does the Negress lay claim to her own life, as the narrator of Elizabeth

Hardwick's novel *Sleepless Nights* does: "It is June. This is what I have decided to do with my life just now. I will do this work of transformed and even distorted memory and lead this life, the one I am leading today."

The Negress in literature is a nearly dead construct who does not exist independent of her creator's need to fulfill his or her audience's expectations of performing "black" writing. She is a necessary component in the building of a black writer's career: she signifies "oppression" and, by extension, blackness; she is never complex, or rich, enough to be fucked up. If the matriarchal society the Negress represents—in fact, and in these authors' imaginations—is so despised, she should be killed off along with it. But Wideman and Alice Walker, among others, are too admiring of their egos on the page, and depend on the Negress's presence too much, to unravel how they are bound to her, for fear that without her, they'd have no careers whatsoever. They keep the lid shut tight on the Negress's curly Medusa head and go on speaking, uninterrupted.

Also: they make the Negress bigger than she is in order to mythologize her. As a myth, she does not have to be complex or subtle. She is larger than life, like Pilate in Toni Morrison's *Song of Solomon*. She is uglier than life, like Celie in Alice Walker's *The Color Purple*. And she appears to superb theatrical effect from time to time, especially when her presence represents someone else's failure of expression, as in the late British author John Osborne's *The Entertainer*:

Archie: Do you know the most moving thing that I ever heard? It was when I was in Canada—I managed to slip over the border sometimes to some people I knew, and one night I heard some Negress singing in a bar. *Now you're going to smile at this*, you're going to smile your educated English head off, because I suppose you've never sat lonely and half stewed in some bar among strangers a thousand miles from anything you think you understand. But if ever I saw any hope or strength in the human race, it was in the face of that old fat Negress getting up to sing about Jesus or something like that. She was poor and lonely and oppressed like nobody you've ever known. Or me, for that matter. I never even liked that kind of music, but to see that old black whore singing her heart out to the whole world, you knew somehow in your heart that it didn't matter how much you kick people, the real people, how much you despise them, if they can stand up and make a pure, just natural noise like that, there's nothing wrong with them, only with everybody else. . . . There's nobody who can feel like that. I wish to God I could, I wish to God I could feel like that old black bitch with her fat cheeks, and sing.

One of the more powerful examples in contemporary literature of the black American author's fear of the Negress is *The Autobiography of Malcolm X*. In it, Malcolm expresses his physical horror at the Negress from the start. Besides categorizing the Negress as a culturally and racially different species, he makes palpable and personal his physical repugnance at her difference by identifying the Negress he would destroy if he could: his mother, Mrs.

Louise Little. "My mother, who was born in Grenada, in the British West Indies, looked like a white woman. Her father *was* white. She had straight black hair, and her accent did not sound like a Negro's." In the *Autobiography*, Malcolm inflates the part of Mrs. Little he hated, feared, and admired—her whiteness—which, in turn, propelled his career as a "militant" black nationalist into being. Even so, he could not help projecting his face onto his mother's: "My mother . . . looked like a white woman . . . I looked like my mother." The *Autobiography* is a primer on how not to write about the Negress—that is, from the small and banal vantage point of the monstrous ego that prevents her from living on the page.

I began trying to pry Mrs. Little out from under the *Autobiography* by imagining: What if one did not write about her as a mother at all, but as Louise adrift in Grenada, in what was then the British West Indies, in her crepe de chine dress—her only one—making her way to America? What if one tried to unearth the reasons behind Mrs. Little's emigration from Grenada to America? Malcolm is short on the biographical details of his mother's life, since he can only see Mrs. Little as the more complicated reflection of himself. And he obscures the powerful emotional energy Mrs. Little may have resonated with by dominating her story with his rhetoric, especially as she takes focus in his memoir as she slides into madness after her husband's murder and, following that, the removal of her children to one foster home or another. She was so alone. What price did she have to pay for her forbearance? And why did she not make the world pay for it, like Malcolm? Malcolm lived less for other people than he did for power. His mother had no choice but to live for other people, being first a woman and then a mother. She was not alone long enough to know herself, emigrating, as she did, from Grenada to Canada, where she met Earl Little, "an itinerant minister," whom she married and settled with, finally, in Lansing, Michigan, in midwestern America. No biographer—including Malcolm—has reported what her age was when she emigrated to Canada. In Canada, what did Earl Little preach as an "itinerant minister"? Was Louise Little charmed by his speech? Was it as mad as Malcolm's? Was Earl Little charmed by Louise's crepe de chine dress as he limped through the provinces, preaching what? Did Louise Little have more language than her husband? No one knew what her presence would mean to the United States and its future. Her emigrating to the States is never explained, let alone described, in the *Autobiography*. She exists in the *Autobiography* to give birth to Malcolm, go mad, and look nearly colorless. What did Louise feel, growing up in Grenada, with its green limes and blue sea, having never (according to Bruce Perry's biography *Malcolm: The Life of the Man Who Changed Black America*) seen her Scottish father during all the time she'd spent there. The dupie that was Louise Little's father hovers happily in the *Autobiography*. He is what Malcolm longed to be—not a Negress, but a male as mythic and powerful as Grandfather. Earl Little is reported to have said to his parents, on the occasion of Malcolm's birth: "It's a boy . . . But he's white, just like Mama!" Malcolm is reported to have to said to Alex Haley, his collaborator on the *Autobiography*: "Of this white father of hers I know nothing except her shame about it."

What is Louise reported to have said about her own father? And of her "shame"? Did she ever describe it as that? And to a child? Malcolm said: "I remember hearing her say she was glad she had never seen him. It was, of course, because of him that I . . . was the lightest child in our family." Was Louise Little glad not to have seen him because she was frightened by Malcolm's more than physical resemblance to her father? Malcolm had so much ambition—was it genetic? And his need for love on his own terms: from whom did he learn just to take it? Grandfather? Grandfather did not wear the mask of piety. In order not to, one must believe in oneself to the exclusion of other people. Malcolm believed in the reality of his experience to the exclusion of all other realities except one: Grandfather, who was a dupie.

Malcolm attached himself to Louise's male, noncolored half. Louise did not have to meet her father; Malcolm lived him by competing with his ghost at every turn. Is that why Malcolm loved and feared his mother? Because she looked like the memory of the power he wanted to possess and eventually did as a world-famous minister of sorts? His success was greater than that of his fake black male construction known as his dad, Earl Little—a preacher who roamed the provinces "spreading the word of Marcus Garvey" in the early 1920s in one place after another.

Malcolm held Louise Little's father responsible for his mangled consciousness and, indirectly, for the eventual absence of Earl Little, who was dark-skinned and ineffectual—unlike Malcolm or Mrs. Little: ". . . I was among the millions of Negroes who were insane enough to feel that it was some kind of status symbol to be light-complexioned. . . . But . . . later, I learned to hate every drop of that white rapist's blood that is in me." I am sure Malcolm did not mean this literally. First of all, how do we know Louise Little's mother was raped? How do we know that Louise Little's mother—who is not mentioned in the *Autobiography* at all—did not love Louise's father? How do we know that Louise Little's parents did not meet on the side of a road in Grenada? And that Mrs. Little's future parents were not both on foot? How do we know they didn't hear the sound of crickets or a mongoose's stuttering run and, being frightened of both, Mrs. Little's mother didn't collapse into her father's arms—a gesture of trust which Louise Little's father was grateful for? In pausing to look at one another, did they pause to consider the eventual outcome of their meeting: Louise Little, Louise Little in America, Louise Little in America producing Malcolm? Louise Little's life is a series of sentences that amount to a question.

Does history believe in itself even as it happens? Malcolm wrote: "I feel definitely that just as my father favored me for being lighter . . . my mother gave me more hell for the same reason. She was very light herself. . . . I am sure that she treated me this way partly because of how she came to be light herself." Which was? "Her father." In every sentence of the *Autobiography*, Malcolm is attempting to dismantle that fake construction known as the black male—his dad, Earl Little—especially as he clings to what his ideology would call Earl Little's "adverse, negative oppressor": Grandfather, the dupie. Malcolm knew next to nothing about his mother's culture; in any case, he had to struggle against their sameness if he was going to survive Negressity as a man. What resonated for Malcolm most about his mother's past was the fantasy of Grandfather, his "rape." It is clear Malcolm may have been attracted to the potential fantasy of Grandfather as rapist because it endowed Grandfather with the power Malcolm needed to emulate in order to learn how to take and take in this common world.

Mrs. Little was "smarter" than Mr. Little. Malcolm said: "My father and mother . . . seemed to be nearly always at odds. Sometimes my father would beat her. It might have had something to do with the fact that my mother had a pretty good education." Malcolm disliked his mother's intelligence because he admired it. For him to admire it without malice would have been to accept his own nature as a Negress, which he could not do in order to be that figment of his imagination—a black male. He admired his mother's mind in the way he admired most things—with loathing and fear, if he couldn't control it. Malcolm said: "An educated woman, I suppose, can't resist the temptation to correct an uneducated man. Every now and then, when [my mother] put those smooth words on [my father] he would grab her." Being intelligent made Mrs. Little feel different. Being intelligent made my mother retreat into silence so that other people wouldn't feel entirely different from her. Did Mrs. Little ask, by speaking, to be punished? Is that how she lost her mind? The famous photograph of Malcolm in his house with a gun, looking out the window—I believe he is on the lookout for his mother. Looking out that window, did he see his mother's quite appropriate anger, based in part on the fact that in the *Autobiography* he refers to her as Louise while Bruce Perry refers to her as Louisa? What *was* her name? Her date of birth? What parish in Grenada was she born in? When Malcolm looked out that window, did he see his mother holding a diary? What was written in it? Mrs. Little did not write: He did not know my name. He could not bear my presence. What would Mrs. Little have written? She didn't write anything that has been "rediscovered." I am writing the *idea* of Mrs. Little, with practically nothing to base it on.

Therein lies the paradox of trying to create an *Autobiography* Mrs. Little can inhabit. Since I am not capable of writing about the Negress without seeing myself, I cannot discuss Mrs. Little without seeing myself in her narrative—not unlike Malcolm. My portrait of Mrs. Little would not be objective. But there would be attempts at objectivity in it from time to time, as in my being able to surmise and delineate how Malcolm showed his endless fascination with his mother. He showed it in his violent attempts at Negress avoidance. Malcolm writes of the effect his father's death had on his mother, but only as it reverberated for him: "We began to go swiftly downhill. The physical downhill wasn't as quick as the psychological. My mother was, above everything else, a proud woman, and it took its toll on her that she was accepting charity. And her feelings were communicated to us." Malcolm can't imagine what the emotional truth of the following may have meant to Mrs. Little: ". . . I remember waking up to the sound of my mother's screaming again.

. . . My father's skull, on one side, was crushed in, I was told later. . . . Negroes in Lansing have always whispered that he was attacked, and then laid across some tracks for a streetcar to run over him. His body was cut almost in half."

Mrs. Little lost her mind for political reasons, in a sense. When Mrs. Little lost her mind, she was perhaps not quite ready to relinquish the idea of that construct known as a husband, onto whom the Negress displaces her dreams and her will. When that construct no longer exists for the Negress, does she go mad trying to hold in what her shadow-husband once absorbed? Perhaps that was one reason for my mother's illness: after my father left, she had to create another body that could absorb her dreams and will. My mother constructed something far stronger, more reliable and controllable than a husband; she developed a body founded on pain; it was the only thing she knew that could further withstand the self-punishment and hope her mind would inflict on it at every turn. Malcolm became the body Mrs. Little needed to absorb her fear and confusion after Earl Little's death, but Malcolm couldn't take it, being too full of the fear and resistance in regard to the Negress that defined many of his actions.

As Mrs. Little went mad and Malcolm became more famous, Malcolm visited her from "time to time" in the state mental hospital at Kalamazoo, where she was committed—by whom?—for twenty-six years. She existed there, Malcolm says, in "a pitiful state" as her son roamed the world. What was her bed like in that institution? What did Malcolm speak of to this woman? Did other inmates call her Madame X or Mrs. Little? When he saw her face,

did he see his own? Did she slap him? "She didn't recognize me at all. . . . Her mind, when I tried to talk, to
reach her, was somewhere else. . . . She said, 'All the people have gone.' " Gone where? Malcolm did not ask. Did
he attempt to convert her? Was it too late? Did anyone
place a sheet of paper before her? A pencil? She did not
write the book we need. Mrs. Little survived her son—
insane, by all accounts, but she survived him. Did she read
his book? Did she find herself missing from it? Did she
consider writing her own? She could have followed the
tenets of "black" writing, repeating the same story over
and over again for audience approval—a story that in-
cludes Mom wearing the mask of piety, and what have
you. Did Mrs. Little believe her son's book could not be
surpassed? Did she ever possess the confidence to believe
she could smash the mask of piety that was forced over
her face as a Negress by writing its destruction down? She
was a mother, and therefore responsible for the life of her
children, one of whom did write her life down, but for
himself, not for her, and in scraps, and falsely.

The *Autobiography* remains a hit because it has all the
elements that make most black writing as performance
successful—a Negress driven mad by her husband's murder, the dust of patriarchy, religious conversion into the
sublime—and yet it gives nothing, including intimacy.
How could it be rewritten by Mrs. Little, a Negress who
did not look like one? Could she create an *Autobiography*
rich in emotional fiber, with a love of God and children
and so forth?

Consider Louise Little's story inside the model of the
Autobiography. Malcolm's book begins:

Chapter One: Nightmare

When my mother was pregnant with me, she told me later, a party of hooded Ku Klux Klan riders galloped one night. Surrounding the house, brandishing their shotguns and rifles, they shouted for my father to come out. My mother went to the front door and opened it. Standing where they could see her pregnant condition, she told them that she was alone with her three small children, and that my father was away.

Louise Little would have been incapable of writing nothing but anger and confusion. She was a Negress.

If Louise Little had written the above, would she have written: I am fat. When I opened the door to my home in Lansing, Michigan, one evening, some men saw me and my children. Could the men see I ate food replete with many empty calories? In a fat body, did I appear self-sufficient to some, a mountain of solace to my husband and children from which they took as they grew? Could they see I required nothing in return? I'll go mad if I continue to say I require nothing.

Would Mrs. Little have written: Long before I stood at the door to my home in Michigan, I was in the West Indies, standing in the sun. I became a mother lost to history, driven partially mad with love for my children. In Grenada, I was a young woman with broad feet curled in gray or yellow sand; later, my feet curled around my husband. I wore dress shoes two sizes too small. Eventually my son, Malcolm, killed me with his language. Now, I lie dead upon the verbal catafalque he created and he sits in my death still, resembling every inch of my face, speaking loudly, hating everything, saying nothing.

Like my sister, I grew up to lie with first one man and then another, or, more accurately, to bend over one man and then another in parked cars that lined the piers on the West Side Highway. Until the end, I avoided recounting these facts to my mother. I avoided explaining the impetus that propelled me to leave my mother's home in Brooklyn for the piers on the West Side Highway. I avoided explaining that I had been motivated to sit in parked cars with one man and then another by the same desire and romantic greed that had propelled her to move from Barbados to Manhattan. I avoided explaining that when I sat in parked cars with one man and then another, I felt closer to my mother's experience of the world than I ever did in my mother's actual presence. I avoided recounting how I met other Negresses like myself on the piers. I avoided mentioning how those other Negresses were like me, the boy children of women who had emigrated to New York from islands like Jamaica, Cuba, Antigua, Anguilla, Barbados, Barbuda, to find themselves in New York with bad men and children swollen with need. I avoided recounting how some of the Negresses I knew on the piers manifested their need: how M. spent much of his time gagging on the cocks he took down his throat until he vomited, which was his fetish; how K. went to one bar where men with dull eyes pissed on him. I also avoided mentioning that what most of us Negresses were looking for on the piers was that construction known as male, necessary for shutting our Negress selves down.

I avoided mentioning how, as we looked for those men, we would stop in bars and play the jukebox, which emitted songs with words that said more about our desire than we could ever say.

I avoided mentioning telling those men in parked cars how, even though language was powerfully present in my home, it was rarely evoked, and how we lived in an atmosphere of High Anglican style, and a nearly baroque silence. I avoided mentioning how the men I seduced were almost always white, because I did not visually associate their color with anything that mattered, such as Negressity, home, my mother.

I avoided recounting how, with my mouth tentatively poised over one man's mouth and then another's, I sometimes thought: I am not my mother; this is *my* story. I sometimes thought: If she knew that I was performing this act, this gesture, she would perhaps die, releasing me to live fully in the moment. Removing my mouth, I sometimes thought: This is my life; I am a Negress and I will suffer because of my pleasure. I will live a narrative of my own devising—one that competes with my mother's. I avoided recounting how, when one man or another would hold me, I would remember how my mother was about to be ill and how my father might have cared for me if I were ill. Like my sisters, I was a Negress. As a child, I had yet to adopt being a good neighbor as my social way of being. As this man, or another and another, would fondle me, I did not think: This is what love is: the perpetual struggle to try to recapture what the heart responded to as the Good, maybe once, long ago.

And I avoided recounting how, when we left those cars and bars in our soiled blue jeans, after the long subway ride home to Brooklyn or Queens or the Bronx, we were met, at the kitchen door, by our mirror image, Mom, a Negress, who rarely recounted anything about her life at all.

Because my mother spent most of her time dying, many women she knew—my father's sisters, my sisters, one or two of her neighborhood friends—created a circle around the event of her long-anticipated death. These women knew there was power in it. Some of them even co-opted it as the greatest event, the greatest story of their lives. These women marveled at the defeat and loss, the bitterness and recrimination, the silence and cunning, the love and generosity, that my mother, living and dying, had borne with the alacrity of a stoic. In their lives, these women had experienced similar emotions, but had tried to obfuscate them with the vows of motherhood and marriages which no illusionary veil could obscure the pain and boredom of. To these women, my mother was a kind of Cassandra, who saw their future as well as her own. What they saw in my mother was a woman who, having disavowed the conventions of marriage, chose to control her own demise instead. I have yet to stop considering either as life's only options.

The central link in this circle of women was my father's sister, who remains the first Negress I ever knew who did not avoid recounting the facts of her life. My mother was attracted to her because of this, but she also shied away from my aunt's speech; it made my mother's silence more pointed and my aunt's Negressity more entertaining. My aunt had already established her presence in the world by becoming a dramatic alcoholic. When I went to stay with her—generally when my mother was in the hospital for one thing or another—I would watch her turn large and green with alcohol. Her alcoholism was the event of her life, and it dwarfed the emotional life of those around her: her widowed mother, her husband, her daughter, my father, and (sometimes) me.

My aunt made up her internal physiognomy far too garishly; and her rouge pot consisted of violent language. Like the poets my sister would eventually introduce me to in Harlem, she was too rhetorical in her stance. There was no way into her language, but her performance resonated for her audience. She poured glass after glass of scotch and the brown liquid gurgled as her large eyes became larger, then her neck, and then her entire body. She observed the events of her life as if from a great distance— that distance being the land spit of her mind and body. And as I observed her—the way my mother sometimes did—she became literature: that is, she took on the contours of a figure who could engage my imagination. She was a Negress. She drank to forget the fact that she felt dwarfed by my father's exceptional beauty. She drank to mourn her older sister's renunciation of a promising career as a jazz musician because their father had told her that

playing jazz is for whores. She drank because her 'second
child, a boy, was born dead—twenty years before I knew
her—and I, who was alive, was named after him. She
drank when she suggested that she "killed" him. She
drank because her mother had not wanted her to be born.
She drank because she was a woman. She drank because
she was a nurse. She drank because of the fecklessness of
men, the despair of all women, and the fact that she could
not write her language and somehow claim her life—it
was too oratorical, too rhetorical.

So she replaced her life with its mundane exigencies.
Every day of her married life, she argued with her husband
about what he had not turned out to be, what her daughter would turn out to be ("a bitch"), how the world had
turned against her. She had the gift of language, but she
couldn't use it. Her drinking brought forth the sense that
language had turned to waste in her twilight mind, which
lived in the past while she went on uttering the old, old
female story: her inability to forgive life for what it had
not allowed her to claim: herself.

Until I knew my father's sister, I did not know that class
issues had an effect on the daily life of the Negress. I realized this when I observed that my father's sister and her
daughter had more of most things—money, clothes—than
my sisters and mother had. When I noticed this, I was five,
or twelve; at any rate, I was a child, and impressed by the
glamour of their prosperity. My admiration was made

more delicious by the fact that I experienced economic envy of another Negress. Until then, it had not occurred to me that the Negress world I had been born into was not the entire world. My daily life with my mother and sisters was so different from my aunt's. My mother, my sisters, and I spent a great deal of our time going to the storage bins that families on public assistance were required to go to then, to pick up large tins of ketchup, corned-beef hash, empty calories. We filled up on the empty calories we consumed. A social worker came to our home to find out if my mother worked, or whether she had a boyfriend who helped her financially. I learned how to be a conversationalist as I amused the beleaguered, suspicious social worker while my sisters and brother hid the possessions my mother had acquired through her employers: frying pans, a small black-and-white television set, a typewriter.

My aunt knew very little about all this. She was fat with drink and privilege. As my aunt drank, her eyes took in her possessions and numbered them: the beautiful house with dark wood paneling, heavy drapes, and wooden blinds, all of which my grandmother had acquired through thrift and fortitude, ostensibly for her children, who could not see any surroundings without projecting their despair onto them.

In certain photographs taken at her marriage, my aunt wears a wedding dress of green satin and carries a small

corsage. Copies of the same photograph were on prominent display throughout my grandmother's house. My
grandmother cleaved to achievement of any kind. My
grandmother's children—my aunts, my father—had
achieved nothing in this common world except marriage
and children and maintaining a sense of their own privilege. And alcohol on my aunt's lips could never dispel the
words that tumbled over each other, picking over each
bitterness. When she looked at her wedding photograph,
she saw not how the dress fit her, but its creases.

In the privacy of my home, I consider certain facts: that
my mother died in Barbados, our ancestral home. Before
she left New York for Barbados, I did not visit her to say
goodbye; this was only one of many leave-takings. When
my mother left New York for Barbados, she did not say
goodbye to many people who had known her. My mother
could not bear to say goodbye to anyone, although she
did it continually. I have acquired this tendency of my
mother's without quite knowing how. I have also acquired
her drive to suicide. But I have only shown it once. I had
learned from many years of watching my mother that one
way to join the body and mind together was through suicide. After she died, I tried to kill myself. But I laughed
so hard watching myself do this in the bathroom mirror
that the pills in my mouth spilled out. How could a hand-
ful of pills compare with the years my mother spent dying?

In Barbados, my mother did not say goodbye to her

sister who lives there still. "I knew she wouldn't come back. I knew she would die there," my mother's sister told me when I went to Barbados after my mother's death to see where she had died and perhaps retroactively to spend time with her (I was so lonely knowing her alive; now that she is not alive, she is everywhere, like words). My visit meant nothing to my mother's sister. She is not interested in the facts of anyone's life—a family trait. She said several things when I went to visit her in her ugly house surrounded by coconut trees on a pitiful plot of land. She said: "Your mother was so angry at the end." She asked: "When did you know you were going to be an auntie man?" She asked: "When will you write a story about me?"

I did not ask: Am I not a Negress too? Incapable of making a gift of myself to myself? In that ugly house in Barbados as the trade winds blew, my aunt was telling me I could.

2

One spring afternoon in 1987, a number of men convened in the chapel of the Friends Meetinghouse on East Fifteenth Street for a memorial service. The men were white and, for the most part, gay. As New York-based editors and writers, gallery owners and museum curators, theater directors and performers, fashion designers and interior decorators, investment bankers and CEOs, they had shaped and dominated much of New York's cultural life since the early sixties. On this occasion, their respective worlds converged to honor Dorothy Dean, who had been a significant presence in the gay environs of New York for nearly twenty years. She had died the previous winter of lung cancer. She was fifty-four.

Before seats were taken and the eulogies began, gossip prevailed. Conversation focused on loss as a result of AIDS and on sobriety achieved through AA. Friends who had not seen each other for a while said so. Former lovers were avoided.

And interspersed throughout the conversations was Dean lore, cultivated during her life lived as performance. There were conversations that recalled Dorothy's erudition and moral conscience; there were memories of Dorothy as a confidante and betrayer of confidences.

But there was no conversation among Dean's mourners about the figure she'd become: a shabby metaphor for New York's disenfranchised, whose "unrealized" life became realized in a number of novels—she is Dee Dee Beane, the imperious "mascot of Manhattan" in Darryl Pinckney's *High Cotton*, and she is Gwen, the "black Dorothy Parker," in Lynn Tillman's *Cast in Doubt*—and whose failure is used by her interpreters to exhibit their narrative control over yet another notoriously difficult Negress.

"Dorothy was the kind of character New York used to *breed*," said writer George W. S. Trow, one of Dean's eulogists that afternoon. "Dorothy had access to Warhol before he was Warhol. She had access to the Harvard aspect and the camp aspect. It's difficult to imagine an African-American woman in a comparable social role today."

Relatively few of the mourners knew Dean had earned a BA with honors in philosophy from Radcliffe in 1954 and a master's degree in fine arts from Harvard four years later. Or that she had been a Fulbright scholar in Dutch and Flemish painting. Or that she had been the first woman fact checker at William Shawn's *New Yorker*, or a copy editor at Huntington Hartford's *Show* magazine, and at *Vogue*, and at *Essence*, which Dorothy called "the magazine that proves black is *pathetic*," and, following all that, a freelance copy editor for a number of book publishers. Or that she had produced and appeared in Andy Warhol's seminal 1965 underground film *My Hustler*. Or that she had been an accomplice in a famous kidnapping case. Or that she had also appeared in a gay porno film directed by avant-garde playwright Jean-Claude Van Itallie called *American Creme*. Or that she had been a woman the writer Jane Kramer recalls as being "the most morally clear person I have ever known." Or that she had written an article about bookbinding for *The New York Times* and many short pieces for *Films in Review*. Or that she had served as an unofficial historian of New York's mid- to late-twentieth-century gay world.

In the end, most of Dean's mourners knew her, simply, as a cynosure in an influential demimonde, a fixture in an era of dramatic social change. For nearly two decades, Dean had reigned, with both cruelty and compassion, over that site of urban gay culture she called "the fruit stand." When she arrived in New York from Cambridge, Massachusetts, in 1962, openly gay bars were as much an anomaly as openly gay men. In 1980, when Dean left New York—or, as she called it, Scum City, Puke City, or Scumsville—to take up residence in Boulder, Colorado, AIDS and gay activism had already begun to lay waste to her world.

"She was our Misia Sert," the architect Buddy Mear says. "And lots of queens are still dining out on Dorothy stories. She's still a major presence."

And it is her galvanizing presence that the late Robert Mapplethorpe, another Dean acolyte, captured in his

1978 portrait, which was displayed on an easel in the lobby at her memorial service. In it, Dean has the demeanor of an ecstatic magistrate, sitting in what appears to be a seat of justice or an electric chair. Her face is electric with intelligence. Her diminutive frame is made vibrant by the event of being photographed. It is a measure of Dean's social importance that Mapplethorpe photographed her at all. She was not a characteristic subject. She was not beautiful. She did not appear to be fashionable or wealthy or the creator of anything important outside herself. She was not a black man.

But she was a symbol whose death signaled an end to *their* era, which, from our unremittingly correct, grided, ahistorical present, has come to represent a time of highly aestheticized waste. The beginning of Dean's social fame (the early sixties) can be seen in images recorded by photographers Stephen Shore and Billy Name and Bob Richardson, images that reflect the gracility of many of the era's participants, but not what distinguished them: they were the last generation of young, urban, educated Americans to treat language as a vital means of communication and the first generation of young, urban, educated Americans to disavow language as a means of communicating anything at all. By the time of Dean's death, her generation was slowly being replaced by the new gay politics that regarded the excesses and social mores of the sixties and seventies—drinking, drugs, sexual experimentation, fag hags, language, the twin recourse of flamboyant display and closeted furtiveness—as dead, or nearly so, as many of its participants.

.   .   .

Dean was born into the black bourgeoisie in 1932. Her father, the Reverend Elmer Wendell Dean, was a native of Statesville, North Carolina. He made his way North and eventually led congregations in New York and New Jersey. For a time, he settled, with his wife and their two daughters—Dorothy and her older sister, Carol—in White Plains, New York, where the girls attended high school.

As members of the black middle class, Dean's family stressed the importance of academic achievement. Scholarship was considered essential in the construction of a self that went beyond being "just" colored and female. Growing up, Dorothy was touted by her family and their friends as exceptional. (She was the first black valedictorian in the history of White Plains High School.) As an exception, she had to be as clean, polite, puritanical, and ladylike as possible. As an exception, she had to rise above comments like the one Dean's high school English instructor made in his letter recommending her to Radcliffe: "[Should I] encourage a brilliant . . . little negro girl to think of Radcliffe as a possible fairy godmother?" As an exception, she could not risk being ordinary. In order not to be "just" colored and female—a Negress—Dean had to maintain emotional and social distance from those blacks who were not of the same social or economic standing. (In a 1959 letter to Dean, her sister referred to a group of blacks living near their mother as the "Spook Menace.")

"You are no ordinary person," Dean's mother wrote to her in 1969, urging her to apply for a job as the "Negro faculty person in the Admissions Office at Swarthmore College," adding: "You are a negro cum laude graduate of one of the best colleges in the world. Valedictorian of a top High School, in a class of over 500 graduates."

Despite the overt racism and discrimination of the fifties, many American middle-class blacks prospered during the postwar boom. Many of the Deans' friends were self-employed and had small businesses within the black community or owned real estate. Others had careers in black-run colleges or the church. Their world was small and insular, and Dorothy hated it. She called most blacks "niggers." She referred to writer and civil rights activist James Baldwin as "Martin Luther Queen." In *The All-Lavender Cinema Courier*, a newsletter she wrote and published in the seventies, Dean criticized one black film as "a disgrace to the race, and I do mean jigaboo . . . I think it is shocking that the likes of Billy Dee Williams and the Big Black Dope himself, i.e. James Earl Jones, should lend their services to such a project and I would venture to opine that it merely goes to show that spades are every bit as venal and rapacious as anybody else when it is a question of money. Step right up, darkies, and gits your watermelon here."

Dean did not reject her social class (she was comforted by the *idea* of these two constants: privilege and hierarchy); what she did try to reject was her parents' proto-black politics, which included being made to feel, intellectually, that one was emotionally responsible for other blacks simply because they were black—a thought process that involves no thought at all, but a dull reaction. And one way of reacting against the dead and deadening ideology (inspired by Booker T. Washington by way of W. E. B. Du Bois) that her parents embraced was for Dorothy to become a disgrace to the race. She began doing so by being candid about her reverence of white people, whom her family (secretly) considered the Good and whom Dorothy never considered complex. Which was convenient if she was eventually going to act out her Negress-as-performance in the company of white people who didn't know how to define it as such. Dean was very little interested in being "understood," just as, from a very early age, she had very little interest in anything outside her internal world that didn't provide some form of resistance.

Dean could never entirely separate from the stultifying confines of her respectable Negressity. (Her lifelong belief in ostentatiously genteel modes of address, speech, and nicknames began at home. Dean addressed her parents in letters as the Furries; her grandfather Cornelius as the Old Bear.) Nor would she approach, let alone embrace, aspects of Negro culture that more or less defined her self (she called rock and roll "screaming nigger fuck music"). Away from home, at Radcliffe, she chose her own oppression. "I am a white faggot trapped in a black woman's body," she used to say. As an undergraduate, Dean began attracting men who would meet her parents' standards, given that they were white, moneyed, with access to power. Unlike the Deans, the men Dorothy courted had a complicated relationship to what they were: white, moneyed, with access to power. Nevertheless, those men were like Dorothy in one respect: they were a disgrace to their privileged race because they were homosexual. They were also like Dorothy in that they were essentially provincial-minded people made socially interesting because they were repressed. Their repressed selves resulted in bodies that projected dread. Their dread centered on their environ-

ment and women. Dean pursued her attraction to these men with a vengeance; one can see Dean reasoning her way toward their value-laden world and "high" aesthetics in her undergraduate thesis, "The Philosophical Foundation of Aesthetic Criticism":

> But it is to be pointed out that from the recognition of critical disagreement as resulting from the use of different standards, it does not necessarily follow that one must assume that all competent critics ought to or must present uniform and correct evaluations. The fact that standards are different need not necessarily lead to the conclusion that only one of them is "correct." As I understand it, the term "correct" applies in these matters, if at all, to judgments based on both sound theoretical foundations and standards met within the history of criticism that might be acceptable either from the point of view of being easily verifiable or from that of being theoretically sound, but not both.

Despite the sophistication of her thesis, Dean did not develop her own voice as a writer. In much of her writing, her voice is self-consciously authoritative, as if she's performing what she assumes to be the role of a scholar. Her work is almost always based on the parameters set by someone else's authority. (Along with a number of other scholars' work, the eminent critic E. H. Gombrich's writings are listed in her bibliography as source material.) Still, it is also possible to find places in Dean's thesis where one

can feel her pushing against the parameters set by recognized authorities; it's as if she wouldn't have much to say
at all if she didn't struggle against the resistance their work
and authority provided.

Dean's thesis is also a window into the value-based but
purportedly objective stance she would would maintain in
the social environs of Cambridge and New York, capable
of "reading" most people but not "just" anyone. Aspects
of this performance included projecting certain European
modes of behavior—a distanced, "objective" stance,
which is an impossibility, or a performance—as well as
being a snobbish Negress who regarded the white world
of privilege as the Good and whose fairy godmother happened to be gay men. Dean was only interested in those
men who were as aesthetically pleasing to her and as frozen in the perfection of their appearance as the Flemish
art she eventually studied and categorized, as a slide li-
brarian at the Boston Museum of Fine Arts, where she
worked for fourteen months in the late fifties, and as a
curator of slides in the Art Department at Brandeis University, where she worked for two years after receiving her
degree in fine arts from Harvard in 1958. As with most
intellectuals, Dean was interested in where her mental
computation could take her. Her choice of companions
validated her mind but not her physicality. The principal
attraction between Dean and the gay men she had begun
to seek out in Cambridge was language, but language as
a tool to obscure intimacy and enforce distance. One's
internal world is never language-based, and if it is, that
language is baroque and not academic in tone, which Dorothy's written work always was. Dean and her male com-

panions tried to communize their language of isolation through academic study and drinking parties, but at its core this language was emotionally noncommunicative, since it had been cultivated in their childhood rooms, where books and an interest in aesthetics supplied the metaphors that approximated their feelings but could not describe them or be made to express them.

Dorothy's male friends lived within the conundrum of being queer and privileged. And it was out of their need to distance themselves from this conundrum, which their collective background would not let them forget was a problem (an interesting aspect of being born to power is how it makes you very aware, from an early age, of where you are positioned in the world—and who might want to usurp it), that the fags Dean courted developed social speech that was ironic and bitter and not imaginative; their speech could not be imaginative because they were children of privilege, who are condemned to know, at all times, where they are positioned—an awareness that squelches the imagination.

They had acquired that bitter tone of voice as a means of conveying several things: their disdain for the straight world of their parents; their smug admiration for the rites and locutions of their class and background and education, which they displayed by exaggerating proper pronunciation; distancing themselves from women. While their desire identified with women because women desired men too, their dislike of women was partially based on the fact that no matter how much money and power they had, they could never garner "real" male interest—or

compete with women for it, being fags, which they regarded as being less interesting than being women.

But since they were men in relation to language—which
is to say self-consciously "objective" and imperious—they
considered their criticism of girls to be legitimate, simply
because they didn't trust them. Also: women represented
what they could not be wedded to in order to be legiti-
mized by the world. They regarded themselves as having
"failed" women and thus the world. Their bitterness was
leveled at the world because it had women in it. They
found no reason to distance themselves from Dorothy, because she created the illusion that she was already distant,
far more so than they had ever been—or could ever access.
Which was compelling. And as if taking her cue from her
audience about the kind of performative Negress she
should be, Dorothy set about proving how little emotional
interest her male companions had in women by being a
self-consciously difficult Negress, ripe to be scorned, awful, with a mind made sordid by the Negroes' fundamental
lack of trust in the white world even as they romanticize
it.

And while Dorothy could be distant from everything,
she could not maintain distance from the young men she
met and loved, because they were herself. But the fundamental difference between the fags Dorothy cultivated and
the Dorothy they courted was this: she could imitate the
sound of an authoritative voice, but not its emotional distance. Just like a woman. And like many other Negresses,
Dorothy Dean did not believe European beauty was separate from value; nor did she believe her association with

their beauty could be valueless. Almost without exception, the men Dean was closest to in Cambridge resembled the works her eye revered.

Dean was not particularly at ease with phenomena that could not be defined by literal description, hence her propensity for describing people "as they were"; she ignored most attempts at self-presentation, instead preferring to control people who feared her powers of critical description, a cruelty that was partially fueled by Dorothy's never attempting to be recognized as a serious scholar in her own right. Rather, she preferred the safety of being a bitter baby, a babyhood that grew and grew as her complaints about her lack of ambition grew; she nursed on apathy. She was as loyal to all this as she was loyal to her self-consciously adopted and relished role as secretary to great and scholarly men like the art historian Sydney Freedberg, whose two-volume study of Italian Renaissance painting and sculpture Dean typed and edited, and for which she earned a line of thanks in Freedberg's acknowledgments.

The discipline inherent in cataloguing and studying the minute detail that goes into producing a "masterpiece" of beauty can produce a person with a mind that is generally perceived as authoritative, sharp, disinterested, incapable of being made banal by "feeling." In his classic study of art historian Anthony Blunt, George Steiner describes the art historian's process of intellection as being informed by a kind of "bizarre violence" in that "the practice of devoting one's waking hours to the collation of a manuscript, to the recension of watermarks on an old drawing," can "secrete a rare venom into the spirit." Then: "Because their constant focus is antiquarian and archival, [art historians] can infect their adepts with a queer, lifeless brand of detestation. . . . The violence stays formal." The formal violence of Dorothy's speech acted as the code by which her male friends recognized themselves. But what made Dean's speech and presence so memorable were the ways in which she leveled her violence at a world that included them; she had very little patience for their confusion over not being the true heirs to their kingdom, because they were queer. She disliked other people's nostalgia for what they might have been. As a Negress, Dorothy was less interested in the ineffable than in drawing conclusions about the real.

When she began her graduate studies at Harvard in 1956, Dean became more closely associated with the loosely formed clique of white gay men she dubbed "the Lavender Brotherhood." She served as their confessor, adviser, and cruise director. As a socially authoritative figure, Dean took control of a group of men who had largely grown up in environments where everything was allowed and encouraged, and never controlled by women. Dean's was the first female admonitory voice they had ever known. (Her brief appearance toward the end of *My Hustler* was a send-up of her by then well-known hectoring voice—as well as being a send-up of her family's nostrums about education. Offering advice to the film's male star, Dean says: "You are very pretty but you are not exactly *literate*.

Sweetie, I will get you educated. . . . I mean, why be tied down to these old faggots?")

The Brotherhood would meet Dean for daiquiris at the famous Club Casablanca on Brattle Street. "The Casa B was an atmospheric place, and the sentimental music, the darkness . . . all helped the milieu. . . . It was like being in a theater: someone would make an entrance," said the late writer John Anthony Walker in Jean Stein's *Edie*. At the Casablanca, Dean regaled the Brotherhood with her skill as a verbal caricaturist, cutting like a scalpel into what she called "the soft white underbelly of Cambridge." On those occasions, she was known as Nurse Dean. Or—when she ostracized those who were out of favor—as Dottie Doom. On being introduced to a man who had rented a flat below a friend she was angry with, Dean once said: "I hear you live beneath contempt." She often renamed the members of the Brotherhood; if she was attempting to become something other than herself, they must too. (It was a habit she continued in New York, where she dubbed John Loring, now design director of Tiffany's, "John Boring"; Andy Warhol "Drella" (a combination of Cinderella and Dracula); and Peter Prescott, a founding editor of *Food and Wine* magazine, "Priscilla Puccini.") "She organized café society, or what passed as such, in Cambridge," the writer Tony Hiss says.

Although the Brotherhood was an antidote to the intensely straight and closeted world Harvard fostered in the late fifties and early sixties, few of its members truly rejected their families' values, or Harvard's. ("By then, Harvard was less interested in academics than in the world outside—namely, gaining access to the Kennedys and the political world," a former Harvard student recalls.) The Brotherhood's precepts had generally been established by their parents: cocktails, noblesse oblige, and no political discussion. "The racial attitudes at Harvard, to say nothing of the sexual, were Edwardian, and pretty backward then," Hiss recalls. "No one discussed Dorothy's race; they couldn't deal with it. She had to be 'just' Dorothy."

Unlike more than a few of her black American middle-class counterparts, Dorothy refused to take even a perfunctory interest in a politics of oppression she did not own—and could not own her. She would not play the stock narrative of the pastor's daughter heading the local chapter of the NAACP—while consorting with white men on the side. She would not become a proponent of miscegenation while conveniently excluding her personal investment from the argument. And she would not accept being a Negress who was repulsed by black men romantically as a reflection of her own self-hatred. What Dean believed was that intellectual life was a function of being European and male. And one way of ensuring that her identification would be taken seriously was to deny her body everything while indulging in behavior that was gay-male-identified. She drank. She was promiscuous when she was allowed to be. She was authoritative in her knowledge and critiques of most things she did not consider herself to be, which included being a Negress in this common world. "I remember a friend saying to me once, when I asked him what Dorothy's politics were, as a black: 'But Dorothy is white.' And in every respect she was, except the obvious one: her skin color," recalls historian Rollins Maxwell. The film and theater critic John Simon, who met

Dean at Harvard, insists: "I think if anyone had told her she was black, it would have come to her as an astonishing revelation."

As a European engaged in issues of connoisseurship, Dean based her aesthetic philosophy on a form of morality: the beautiful was only possible in people who were unlike herself. In order to become a different self, Dean revered and denigrated the "elevated."

As a member of the Brotherhood, Dean was not officially considered black or female—a Negress. But it was precisely those characteristics that the members of the Brotherhood used to substantiate themselves. They were queer but at least they weren't Dorothy. They could pass in their chosen careers; Dorothy couldn't. As a Negress, Dorothy was viewed as a symbol for the Brotherhood's aberrant sexuality, which they assumed kept them from claiming their full inheritance of unqualified power—a partial truth. What also prevented them from resting comfortably on the mantel of privilege was their sensibility, which attracted them to women like Dorothy, of whom they often took a self-serving and sentimental view. That view did not include any insight into Dorothy's bitterness, which was the outgrowth of her hope, and that her hope was this: that her difference mattered to no one but herself. And this: that her mind mattered in this common world. In the end, the only emotional certainty Dorothy had was her bitterness, just as the only other emotional certainty she'd ever had was her hope that one day she could become something other than herself without having to achieve it.

Dean ironized her position as a metaphor for upper-class queer sexuality and privilege by "out-Wasping the Wasps," says the writer A. J. Sherman, who shared a house with her in Cambridge. She accomplished this through costume (thick glasses, dainty sleeveless shifts, straight-hair wigs, oversized handbags), tone of voice (a lockjawed drawl), arch syntax ("One must make haste to the fairy aerie"), and finishing school manners (although she might have behaved outrageously the night before, she generally sent a thank-you note to her hosts). None of Dorothy's friends knew enough about the history of her sartorial sense to know that these gestures were those of a correct Negress. Or that that style was less the manifestation of wanting to affect the appearance of a Wasp. Rather, Dorothy's dress and elaborate manners were a scrim—the ornamental scrim behind which most Negroes hide their fundamental distrust not only of the white world but of themselves.

Many of Dorothy's friends did not know or face the fact that they regarded her as physically strange and not "natural." "Part of the fear for people was that she knew them better than they knew themselves," a friend recalls. Within the Brotherhood, Dean frequently ignored its precepts. When she did so, she was playing, more or less, the role of the Bad Nigger.

A Negro colloquialism, the "Bad Nigger" is a title traditionally reserved for men, ascribed to those who command the respect of their peers in urban environments by defying authority: social, political, domestic. Generally, the Bad Nigger restricts his defiant nature to a "hood"— a controllable universe. He is verbally and physically fearless in his limited world. He goes to absurd extremes of self-abnegation and disregard in order to prove his point: that if I am capable of committing this violence to myself, imagine what I can do to you.

Very few of Dean's contemporaries could take in what her Bad Nigger style was comprised of: her fake appearance of self-control, which also converged with the punishing self-control she exercised as a fag hag. Bad Niggers are never less than correct in their dress or ideas, which are generally issued with an authority that is meant to be intimidating. Their language is often baroque in its formality. Dorothy mocked her friends' sensitivity to loss. She mocked their whining privilege. She corrected their grammar. She would not shut up. And she took her frustration at not being something other than herself out on those friends she regarded as extensions of herself—their isolation was her own. They were as resolute in that as they were resolute in their masochism when it came to matters of the heart and their emotional selves, which they thought of as "queer." They considered the impulses that propelled their desire into being wrong and punishable by ostracization from what they wanted: the company of straight men who were sometimes black, like Dorothy, and for whose company they sometimes paid, like Dorothy. In this guise, Dean reverted to being the pastor's puritanical, stern daughter who viewed the world through a moral grid—but with a difference. Dean had grown up in a world that posed "us," blacks, against "them," whites—the righteous against the wicked. Now she transplanted that moral structure—an outgrowth of the church, her first home—to gay New York. Gay men were "us," and "them" was everyone else.

As a greedy romantic, Dean made rash decisions based on the belief that the insular world of the Brotherhood would last forever. She made less and less contact with her family; she did not pursue a career. She would not disappoint the world by not being a failure, given what she perceived were the world's expectations of her as a Negress: forbearance and self-abnegation. She assumed that her struggle to repudiate her family's approval was a goal she shared with the Brotherhood. But no matter how different they were, members of the Brotherhood ultimately did not choose lives or careers so far removed from what had always been expected. They could always go home again; Dorothy wouldn't. And she could never rid herself of what she considered to be the proper female expectation: that, as a woman, she *shouldn't* compete for anything she might want or need.

Of the friends and acquaintances Dean made in and around Cambridge, she was closest to Arthur Loeb, whom she met when both were undergraduates. (She was earning money as a typist, and he hired her to type a term paper.) "He was my best friend. I called him *Liebestraum*," she said. ("And when she was pissed she called him *Liebestod*," the writer and translator Paul Schmidt recalls.)

Now the owner of the Madison Avenue Bookstore, Loeb is the son of John Loeb, a philanthropist and founding partner in the investment banking firm Loeb, Rhoades. John Loeb and his wife, Frances, a member of the socially prominent Lehman banking family, were known as one of the most politically and financially powerful Jewish couples in New York. They financed the building of the Loeb Student Center at New York University, the Central

Park Children's Zoo, the Central Park Boathouse, and the Loeb Theatre in Cambridge. Of the Loebs' five children, their eldest son, John Jr., went on to a career in the diplomatic service, and Arthur's twin sister, Ann, married Edgar Bronfman, former president of Seagram.

Physically impaired (he had been born with very little muscle strength in his left arm and leg), Arthur Loeb had always been a person apart. A family friend speaks of him as the diffident son of two forceful parents: "He rebelled against all that. He was quite different; quite sensitive."

By all accounts, Arthur Loeb's years at Harvard were as difficult as those that had preceded them. ("Not that I was a paragon of mental health *myself*," Dean once joked.) Loeb and Dean saw in each other their own cracked or gilded mirror image, the fundamental difference between them being Arthur's money and social prestige, which Dorothy courted. "The German Jews were at enormous pains to deny any otherness," A. J. Sherman says. "Of course, the Loebs were too assimilated to conform to that type, but I always felt there was a similarity between German Jews and the kind of striving blacks Dorothy came from—their concerns about not associating with 'common' blacks, about being 'lighter' than other dark-skinned people who were not as educated."

A Harvard acquaintance of both Dean's and Loeb's remembers the two making quite a study in contrasts: "Dorothy was small and dark; Arthur was tall and pale. Their social personalities were reversed. Dorothy was Arthur's voice in the world. She was tough. But Dorothy accepted Arthur unconditionally."

Loeb accepted Dorothy as well. In 1954, Dean went to

Holland on her Fulbright. On the boat and for a time after docking, Dorothy kept a journal. It is remarkable in its prescience. She was already interested in all the things she would not accomplish. She rarely dated her entries. She wrote:

Friday 17 Sept 1954

Am finally beginning this European "journal," the whole idea having come up largely through the suggestion of Stan Sherman [who was married to Dean's then best friend and classmate at Radcliffe, Claire Sherman]. Obviously, I should have started it much earlier, but procrastination is nothing alien to my nature. . . .

30 August—

sailed from Hoboken, everything having been done at the last minute, primarily as result of lengthy Cambridge visit. The Furries . . . really were marvelous during this trying period. I really must, in some way, demonstrate my appreciation in some more active way. . . . I truly seem incapable though. . . . People certainly varied. Wealthy-looking tourist types, hordes of students, immigrant-looking people, homos, etc., etc. . . . Considerable time spent in thinking mostly about l'affaire Halle and myself. He is certainly right—pretty soon it will be too late. The first step is reform, I think, in re-building of will power, and this alone is hard enough. God alone knows what the future will hold (which is tantamount to saying no one knows). . . . Was really stupid not to have taken advantage fully of Dutch lessons organized by some of the Dutch students aboard. Cabin-mates Joyce Bockel and Ann Jansen seem almost fluent by now. I abhor their religious tendencies. Also they stick together too much. Joyce, especially, takes herself quite seriously. I know I should, to some degree— but how? . . . This more or less calmness, more properly mental lethargy, on my part, really is a great concern in certain moments of acute distress. One simply must go on "not caring" as it were, shuffling along. Yet I do. Reminds me of Plato, and theory that the "bad," or evil, is only ignorance. I can remember when I used to believe this. . . . Was glad there wasn't anyone I really hated to say goodbye to. Am increasingly reluctant to form attachments to people anymore, precisely because of this always eventual having to say goodbye.

And as if to catch herself in what she would refer to as a "cheap" moment, Dean added a parenthetical postscript to the above sentiment: "(A poor habit, from point of view of seeming, and actually being, in part, 'disinterested.')"

While in Holland on her Fulbright, Dean had a brief affair with a musician named Jacques Holtman. When she returned to Cambridge, she was pregnant. She did not have an abortion. She had the child, a boy, and immediately put him up for adoption. "I met her that summer, after she had the baby, when she was in the hospital," Paul Schmidt recalls. "Arthur paid all her medical expenses."

Between them, Loeb and Dean developed many myths,

many secrets. And the stories about their relationship are filled with conjecture. Was it based in part on Arthur's desire to distance himself from his family? (He once asked Dean to marry him.) Was there any truth to the rumor that Arthur's parents tried to pay Dorothy off to stay away from Arthur? (Vincent Crapanzano recalls: "Arthur's father came to see Dorothy and offered her money to not marry Arthur. It was a great deal of money. Dorothy turned him down flat. She was a morally very strong person. She said something like 'I won't marry Arthur because I don't want to. But I won't not marry him because you say don't marry him.' ") And was Dorothy using Arthur for the gifts of money and attention and grand surroundings she so enjoyed? Out of the apocryphal, this narrative emerged: Loeb eventually stopped drinking and Dean did not. And for those who have stopped drinking, optimism becomes a mode one has greater and greater access to through sobriety. Or, at the very least, it is an attitude one tries to maintain while sober. As a drinker, Dorothy had access to optimism only during drinking bouts. To the former drinker, the jokes don't resonate the same as when one was a drinker. In any case, Loeb and Dean stopped seeing each other sometime later in New York. But before she had even left Cambridge for New York, her body had already started to reject joy as "feeling" too much. It was an emotion she could rarely handle physically, given that her body was intent on surviving what she was imbibing.

In a 1956 letter to Dean from a social worker who was handling the adoption of her child, reference was made to Dean's depressed state. "Life is not as bleak and worthless as you say it is, Dorothy." Like other women known for organizing the party—Elsa Maxwell, Dorothy Parker, Edie Sedgwick—Dean did so to avoid her twilight self, an insecure killjoy, dissociated from her body, incapable of sustained bouts of pleasure. Dean developed her own powerful role, despite an extreme temperament that sought confirmation from the world. Her worst suspicion: wherever the party was, she had not been invited.

"The American upper class had its last dance [in the fifties and early sixties]," Jefferson Lewis, who worked with Dean at *The New Yorker*, recalls. "It was the last time the class game could be played, before what we refer to as 'the sixties' happened. As a black woman then, [Dorothy] was not the girl who *could* really be invited to the party."

Organizing her own party instead, Dean made sure it had all the elements of the tragicomic—walkouts, breakups, sexual intrigue. There was romantic love unfulfilled. ("At some point during the course of the evening she might turn to your boyfriend and say, 'Now look here. Are you going to fuck me or not?' " rock promoter Danny Field recalls.) There was a great deal of unbridled drinking. ("Dorothy *invented* alcohol," Peter Prescott says.) There was gossip and backbiting. ("She was very good at detecting the weaknesses of others and exclaiming them. Loudly," Tony Hiss recalls.) And when the drinking finally ended, there was pathos. Dean once wrote: "I was terrified of dying without having been in love."

By the time Dean completed her MA and left Cambridge for New York in 1963, she had completely excluded from her stratosphere of fun those people she did not want to be—not unlike Dorothy Parker dissociating herself from other Jews, or Elsa Maxwell ostracizing the homely or obscure. "I think Dorothy would have liked to be white and beautiful and clever, perhaps a combination of those three things," says Desmond Fitzgerald, the Knight of Glyn, who met Dean in Cambridge in 1960. "She was far more clever and quick than the people she met. Eventually, I think she was incapable of handling her own . . . temperament."

Dean's temperament—by turns combative and puritanical, bitter and angry, humorous and loyal—was theatrical. And her theatricality informed her role as a fag hag. When she moved to New York, fag hags, like the other factions of New York's disenfranchised—trust-fund babies, dinge queens, hustlers, the avant-garde, sycophants to the rich and famous—had yet to establish their own cult of personality—an eighties phenomenon. In the early sixties, women rarely "dropped out" of anything to join the ranks of the subversive; being oppressed does not allow for the privilege inherent in being "radical."

As a self-defined fag hag, Dean did not seek legitimization of her role by calling it something else. She did not become a wife, as Dorothy Parker had when she married screenwriter Alan Campbell, or Linda Lee had when she married composer Cole Porter. Nor did Dorothy follow Vanessa Bell's and Libby Holman's examples by becoming a theatrically silent or overbearing mother. Dean arrived in New York committed to a different kind of ambition: she was to become something other than herself, something not defined by convention. In renouncing the traditionally "female" desires for marriage, children ("rug rats"), forbearance, Dean pursued a road less traveled, bordered on one side by romanticism and on the other by innocence: she was a Negress consumed by her quest for vengeful independence.

As the self-described Spade of Queens, Dean was supported in her witty vilification of all she disliked—other blacks, many women—by the white gay men she revered. For them, Dean was a fag hag of exceptional brilliance. "I am not a fag hag," Dean said once, to Truman Capote. "I am a fruit fly."

Generally, the fag hag comes into being in an attempt to escape her body by identifying with a difference not her own. She becomes a star attraction among men who have limited, if any, sexual response to her (a fact she eventually, inevitably, resents). The fag hag prizes self-control even as she performs outrageous acts. She harbors anger toward her audience for accepting, laughingly, what she does not speak: her fear of romantic intimacy—which she identifies as a potential violence against herself, given the (assumed) proclivities of heterosexual men, their desire and ability to control *her*. As a woman, the fag hag realizes that she is the image of male fear: vituperative, self-hating, controlling, and punishing. She accepts this image as the truth about herself because she believes it to be fundamentally true of other women, with whom she has little, if any, contact. The fag hag operates on the premise that social ambition in the gay world is her only power.

In order for her power to work, however, that world must stay small and controllable.

What gay men see in the fag hag is someone who plays out their narrative of disenfranchisement. She is *them* in the straight world; she is what they used to be, or may be still: silently in love with the straight boy she cannot have. What the fag hag and the faggot share is the propensity to base their personae on fear, vulnerability, and language. In this hothouse environment, they feed off one another; they compare and contrast slights, injuries, their hard, repressed days at the office. This silent man and this voluble woman experience a marriage of sorts. Such a relationship begins as a joke—the first of many. The joke has a ready-made structure: "us" against "them," with them being the world of the "normal." The fag hag's marriage to her constant gay male companion is a marriage sanctified not by physical love but by Humor and Verbal Punishment. Or, rather, humor that arises out of verbal punishment; it is not uncommon to hear the fag hag and her companion refer to one another derisively—emulating the cruel voices of the children they knew in youth—as "You faggot," or "You bitch." In such a marriage, desire is rarely reciprocated, so the anxiety of potential loss that generally propels sexual desire into being defines their relationship.

The drama of potential loss is played out in telling tales out of school, giving away secrets, or other forms of betrayal, which may lead to the breakup of their marriage. Sometimes the fag hag and her companion reconcile, briefly, but the reconciliation rarely works, since it's often based on old affection, and the original bond was based on tension and laughing and gossiping in the moment.

And it's often during the breakup period after such a marriage that the fag hag becomes involved with what she can never have when she's involved in her marriage: the "real" man her gay male friend can never have. Sometimes the gay man becomes involved with what the fag hag can never be: a gay man. Sometimes, the fag hag and her gay male companion never break up, so profound is their fear of the outside world. They coexist in a kind of stasis that is defined by timetables and cultivating particular dislikes about the world at large. They take their meals at the same time, work in the same office space, share similar styles of dress, and have few, if any, friends outside their marriage because no reality other than their own can intrude on their being the custodians of each other's essential truth: a crushing fear of isolation even as they cultivate it. Silently, they blackmail each other into staying with the other by promising each other they will never change. They do not visit the twilight world of bars, with its juke-box and synthetic optimism or depression, a place too filled with people who are not like themselves. And they replace physical intimacy by becoming, in the mind and body, sexless, resigned to the failure of other people who cannot achieve intimacy with them. When the fag hag and her gay male companion eventually die, they are buried looking not unlike one another.

Gay male social ambition has never excluded the possibility of change based on loss—loss of friends who become lovers and end up as neither, beauties whose faces are ruined by time and bitterness, sartorial enthusiasms that quickly become "old," fag hags who outgrow their audience. This sense of loss accounts for the nostalgic tone permeating so many of the gay environs of New York. Dean, on the other hand, could not maintain this emotional timbre. She hated change. She could not be sober. She could not be productive. She could not, in the end, divest herself of her fag hag role. And, like most roles, it was limited. Its basis was a desire to be seen but not held. She embraced her audience from a distance as she stood on the stony precipice of misplaced desire.

As a fag hag, she amusingly and recklessly repudiated those whom she assumed found her undesirable: heterosexual men. "Dorothy was not very attractive," says Desmond Fitzgerald, former husband of Yves Saint Laurent's muse Loulou de la Falaise. And women: Dean had few women friends and was not a feminist. Regardless of how much control she thought she had, Dorothy was never prepared for a member of the Brotherhood to fall in love with someone else. She would respond with rage and recrimination. She would become her former companion's worst fear: the controlling, vituperative woman he abhorred, just as he—when in love—would become the withholding, controlling man she could not forget. "Rationally or irrationally, it is inviolably idiosyncratic of me that I could never find as acceptable as a truly-true friend and individual [someone] . . . emotionally attached to another person, be it girlfriend, psychiatrist, or God knows what . . . Vital communication [is] hopeless," Dean wrote to Fitzgerald in the early sixties. "I have noticed at almost every recent encounter your abstractedness and restlessness concerning this 'girlfriend' of yours and I find it extremely annoying, not because I am 'jealous' or in any way presume to judge of the wisdom of your so indulging

yourself, but rather because you allow yourself to be ob-
sessed with the matter to the point of outright ill-
manneredness, to say nothing of unbecoming tiredness,
imposed upon your dealings with me. I refuse . . . to serve
as either your mother or psychiatric counsellor."

Dean, in fact, wanted to be Fitzgerald's "abhorred" girlfriend herself, and she manipulated his real or imagined
rejection of her into a final judgment against herself. As
she did, also, with critic John Simon. "She broke off our
long-standing friendship when I began reviewing movies,
in the early sixties, and wouldn't take her to as many
screenings as she would have liked," he recalls. "I suppose
there were other women I was attracted to and wanted to
be with. Dorothy was intelligent, but she was not sexually
attractive. So she told me in great detail of my great injustice as a friend. She had a way of lashing out at you
either behind your back or to your face—depending on
whether your face or back was available."

This perceived antagonism with heterosexual men provided Dean with the resistance she needed to argue against
her conventional fantasy of being someone's girlfriend,
someone's Lady Glyn. Self-denigrating about nearly every
aspect of her body, Dorothy replaced it with language,
which she could control. "Loved I you more than truth.
Kindly consider our . . . relationship at an end. Certain
business matters remain: . . . since you offered, the time
might soon come when I will have to ask you for a loan
of money—'for old times' sake' you might acquiesce. . . .
If you cannot understand 'why' all this, *tant pis pour toi*,"
Dean wrote to Fitzgerald in 1963.

"She didn't like what she called LOs, or Love Objects,"

filmmaker Charles Atlas recalls. "When I became involved with her friend Terry Stevenson, the photographer, whom Dorothy had also been in love with, she tortured me all the time. She said I was nothing but a cheap chiseler. I couldn't take it after a while; I slapped her. I knocked her glasses off. But she never bothered me again."

To be a love object herself would mean giving herself up to the folly of romantic love. And potentially under someone else's control. The men who identified with Dean's pain—gay men—were so taken with her process of intellection that physical comfort rarely entered into the "liking Dorothy" equation; intimacy was replaced by chatter, and few, if any, of Dean's male friends had any interest in divesting her of her shield of language. To do so would be to call her vulnerability into question and thus perhaps their own—a frightening possibility in any human interaction. Instead, Dorothy and her friends replaced vulnerability with a kind of emotional stasis, upon which they piled brick upon brick of the same stale joke about their marginalization, their "difference."

"In the early sixties, you never went to restaurants or anything public like that alone. You would be too self-conscious. You had to have a girl. Dorothy was that girl," Atlas recalls.

As that girl, Dean drew a sharp line between her private self and the improvised script her performance followed, a script she wrote on cocktail napkins, on matchbook covers, and in the margins of other people's lives. In her small, newspaper-strewn apartment on Morton Street, which she occupied from 1962 to 1979, Dean saw only the men who would not contradict her isolation. She spent the majority of her time with the now transplanted Brotherhood in New York, which they treated as an outsized Cambridge. "So much less was expected of you then," filmmaker Paul Morrissey says. "And because no one expected much, you had all the time in the world to be smart and entertaining." For her own amusement and that of the Brotherhood, she sometimes contributed to the classic underground gay magazine *Straight to Hell*. At other times, she could be trying. "She couldn't accept the fact that I didn't want to see her home once," Rollins Maxwell recalls. "Mostly what she couldn't accept was the fact that I was living with a guy she hated, like she hated most of her friends' lovers. I left this party that we'd gone to together. The party was uptown, where I lived then. I left the party relatively early because I was exhausted. Dorothy came to my house after she'd left the party. She started ringing the doorbell at some ungodly hour, demanding that I see her downtown, to her apartment in the Village. My boyfriend got out of bed and went downstairs to try to keep her quiet. She attacked him physically. I can't remember what else happened."

Dean's sexual affairs were limited. Occasionally she'd sleep with a gay male friend who used his drunkenness as a pretext to do so. "She always wanted me to fuck her up the ass; she thought that's what boys did in bed," one friend recalls. Sometimes she shared tricks with her male friends. "If I picked someone up, I'd call Dorothy and send them over to her to fuck too, if I said they were cute," recalls Franklin MacFie. "Sometimes the tricks were more or less straight and would want a girl. That was Dorothy." As a rule, Dean's sexual affairs were confined to one-night stands, including one with singer Kris Kristofferson, about whom she was asked in a questionnaire written by *Straight to Hell* editor Boyd MacDonald: "Would you characterize [Kristofferson] as one of the best pieces of ass you ever had, or was he just an extraordinary lay while being an extraordinary Star?" "Was there any promise of romance, or was it frankly just a couple of pieces of meat hooking up for the night?" "What did he do in the sack besides fuck you? Did he suck your nipples or anything else? Did he try to please you, caress your sensitive parts, or was he mainly interested in getting some friction on his dick?"

The world of the gay upper class in the early sixties was small and closeted enough for Dean to control it with her gossip and advice. "She was an echo chamber," Desmond Fitzgerald says. "Everyone" knew Dorothy, and Dorothy knew "everyone," either from Cambridge (Vincent Crapanzano, Danny Field, Jonathan Kozol), from the artistic avant-garde (Andy Warhol, Robert Wilson, Henry Geldzahler), or from something very like "society" (collector Sam Wagstaff, Bowden Broadwater, critic John Richardson).

And everyone admired Dorothy's erudition, which she sometimes used as a means of "vital communication." Or as a tool to condemn rather than expand her world. "Words used well, nowadays, as a rule constitute the last thing that publishers and editors . . . are concerned with,"

Dean wrote of her publishing career. "An inordinate number within this group, of both high and low rank, are intellectually so ill-equipped and narrowly educated ... Professionalism has become outmoded, and those few of us who continue to espouse conscientiousness will soon be obsolete." As a classically trained polymath, Dean knew more than most of her contemporaries about the origins and history of their European-based ideas. She never missed the chance to prove what other people didn't know: "If you need a working text on the subject of friendship, I commend to your attention a re-reading of the *Nicomachean Ethics*," she once wrote to a friend she was angry with.

"What attracted me to Dorothy was that she was attracted to things of the mind—philosophy and art history and so forth," the writer Rollins Maxwell says. In a memorial festschrift for Norman Fischer, who amassed his important collection of postmodern art through funds he'd obtained as a drug dealer, Dean wrote: "What was so interesting about Norman was his mind. The thing he cared most about was *grammar*."

Although the cocktail party remained a common gathering place through the mid-sixties, its emotional tone changed, due, in part, to the increased use of amphetamines. The Brotherhood maintained a collectively "nice" veneer, and New York matched its highly aestheticized version of cruelty with the threat and, sometimes, the promise of physical violence. (Some members of the Brotherhood found an uneasy solace in the muscular arms of black hustlers, with whom they could play at relinquishing power and privilege in a context they still controlled with money or charm—the same gifts they used in courting Dorothy's favor.) "It didn't matter where she was. She was socially quite fearless," a friend remembers. "And it's important to remember that society is based on fear—keeping everything 'nice' and repressed in order to get through the evening. Dorothy wasn't at all like Gail Lumet, Lena Horne's daughter, who was the only black debutante we had at Cambridge. She wasn't polite or beautiful. Also: Dorothy wasn't famous. She hated Gail because of all of those things, so Dorothy became something else. She spent a lot of time and energy and thought intimidating people into realizing that she was special."

As an adult Dean dressed the part. "Everyone tried to look younger," George W. S. Trow recalls. "Not Dorothy. She carried a *purse*." She defined her limits: "I have found it requisite 'in life' to so arrange my daily affairs as perforce not to admit of the intrusion of existentially distracting influences," Dean once wrote. She had no respect for "alternative" anything (Dorothy called Bob Dylan, a companion of her friend Edie Sedgwick, "Fifi Zimmerman"). She did not engage in the synthetic optimism of the time. But partygoing was still a prolonged distraction. Dean's set replaced career ambition with attitude. Many people "were confused between the stultifying fifties and the silliness of the sixties," Tony Hiss says. Without the discipline to establish their own careers, some bottomed out, exhausted by the effort of making up their epoch as they went along: Free Love, Free Angela, Free Your Mind. One's success and impact as a social figure depended on one's energy level, the ability to be outrageous with little if any moral consequences of bad behavior.

But no matter how far Dean went, no amount of social cachet could make her into something other than what she was. In a way, Dorothy thought being a Negress was a conscious decision; she confused it with behaving like one, or whatever she thought a Negress behaved like (self-abnegating? fat? apolitical?). And because she relegated being a Negress to her consciousness, she thought it was a role she could consciously act against. But she didn't. She was always the pastor's puritanical and stern daughter who views the world through a moral grid. Quite often, Dorothy Dean was seen through a moral grid herself—as something strange and archaic because of the way she negotiated her way through this common world: with language—a not popular way of being by the late sixties. In *My Hustler*, which was financed by a friend who wanted to indulge Dean's wish to act in film, Warhol treated Dean's performance as marginal; the film literally runs out while she is still speaking, most of the time in underexposed darkness.

Dean did not play any of her roles without an audience; if she had, she wouldn't have believed she existed. In the nearly exclusively white worlds of fashion, avant-garde art, and publishing, among the debutantes and queens who made up New York's "underground" culture in the sixties and seventies, Dean was an unusual enough presence to attract notice. And she was especially so at *The New Yorker*, where she had secured a job as a fact checker in 1963.

"Back then, *The New Yorker* was a highly self-conscious place, rather like Cambridge," Jefferson Lewis recalls. "It was a wonderful job. I mean, you showed up at eleven and you went to lunch for two hours . . . And of course, she had an IQ that went off the charts. But no particular ambition. She was lazy. And she didn't observe the decorum of the place. She didn't get on with Lillian Ross, who accused Dorothy of using her extensive contacts in film and theater to advance her social career. Dorothy's don't-tread-on-me personality wouldn't allow for the magazine's more . . . difficult, self-conscious writers."

Calvin Tomkins adds: "Oh, my, she made me feel like an idiot. I was working on a story about Rauschenberg and she was my checker. I handed the piece in and she came into my office and said: 'Is this guy on the level? No one's that nice or interesting. This guy's a fraud, not an artist. You've been taken in.' And so on. And, of course, checkers never ventured an opinion about a piece. Never. That was part of the hierarchy of the magazine. So off Dorothy goes to 'check' Rauschenberg and prove me wrong. And she comes back entranced. Bob used to collect people and he collected Dorothy. She became part of his entourage. For a while."

Brendan Gill: "She was absolutely determined to self-destruct here at the magazine. Why she felt so strongly about the magazine, which fostered a very *familial* feeling, I'll never know. She would do something terrible, and run upstairs to my office and exclaim, rather gleefully: 'I'm going to be fired! I'm going to be fired!' And I would say, well, Shawn will never fire you. She felt she could trust me because I was a friend of Desmond Fitzgerald's and Arthur Loeb's. I was the father figure she could confess to and an ally for the next round of mischief-making. She was so beguiling; the pleasure and delight on her face when she knew she could get away with *something*. And, of course, I was wrong; after about a year, Shawn did fire her."

After being fired from *The New Yorker* in 1964, Dean held a number of other editorial positions, including one at *Vogue* and another at Huntington Hartford's short-lived magazine *Show*. She was fired from *Essence*, her last full-time editorial job, reportedly for suggesting they put Andy Warhol on the cover in black face. Dean's subsequent attempts to support herself were limited. She did freelance copy editing, or accepted gifts of money from friends, or from her mother, whom she rarely visited.

In 1975, she sued Robert Gottlieb, then Alfred A. Knopf's editor-in-chief, for "excessive" services rendered on a number of assignments. In a letter to Gottlieb, Dean wrote: "I have noticed (as have certain reviewers, as you must know) numerous unforgivable slips in Knopf books on which I have not worked at all. For example, take a look at *From Julia Child's Kitchen*, p. 599, Chapter XIV heading in very large letters (and this also appears on the contents page, of course): 'Fundaments.' This is preposterous. Does anyone at Knopf know English anymore (let

alone French)? Does anyone care about language at large?
. . . The primary point I have to make, thus, Mr. Gottlieb,
is: *Please* do something fast. Let's face it, Knopf is going
to hell in a handcart."

Gottlieb's response: "I think this additional money is
deserved. Your work went beyond ordinary 'proofreading.' But I can't place as high a valuation on it as you do.
My personal hope is that you will look for, and find, work
more suitable to your talents than proofreading; you are
bound to be disturbed if you limit yourself to this final
stage of things, where, by definition, you must not be able
to exercise your real capabilities. Which is none of my
business to say, but I've said it."

The world Dean had limited herself to was changing. The
ten years following her arrival in New York saw the riots
at Stonewall, the advent of gay liberation and gay focus
groups, the opening of leather bars like the Spike and
S/M bars like the Mine Shaft, the movement of private
sexual politics into the public sphere, and a new kind of
fag hag was inventing herself. She was still chatty, but less
articulate. She did not have to use language as a way to
be a part of gay culture since gay culture was all she had
ever known; her language was used to convey her genuine
disinterestedness in being perceived as a fag hag, or in any
role. Also unlike Dorothy, the new fag hag had less interest in being adult. She didn't drink, but took heroin. She
was more theatrical in her silence.

Her means of securing her independence was also different from Dorothy's. She was interested in the allure she had for men, and used their power as a means of furthering herself through monetary gain, or imparting sexual pleasure. The new fag hag was younger and more beautiful than Dean, less intelligent but more street-smart. She was popularized by fashionable social reporters like Andy Warhol. Her name was Jane Forth or Donna Jordan and she shaved her eyebrows, wore thrift-shop clothing, did not project pathos, and had an interest in other women. Unlike Dorothy, she was not fearful of losing control of her audience. She was less interested in being male-identified than in seeing herself reflected in their adoration.

Dorothy didn't trust to anyone's adoration or love. She preferred to talk to herself, which had always been the case, except that she'd always had an audience, few of whom knew this.

Sometimes she spent long evenings with Jane Kramer and Vincent Crapanzano and their young daughter, so afraid was she to be alone—a fear she disguised as "the opportunity to have a look at my boring domestic life," Kramer recalls. "We had her to Christmas once, because we knew she was alone. She didn't like us knowing that, but she came. Once, at dinner, she sat next to our daughter. Dorothy was complaining, saying how ugly she was. Our daughter said, 'But you're beautiful.' Dorothy turned on her and said, 'What do you know? *You're* ugly,' as a joke. She could be like that."

Sometimes she sat in a gay bar on Second Avenue and Fourth Street, in the early afternoon, crying. Once, the black male lover of painter Bill Rice asked her what was wrong, what troubled her so much, and she said: "You *nigger,* how dare you pry."

Sometimes she drank and fell asleep at other people's parties. Once, she fell asleep in Robert Wilson's broom closet and was discovered there, still asleep, two days after the party had been over.

Sometimes she fell in love, as she did with Harvard alumnus J. J. Mitchell, who was a friend of poet Frank O'Hara, and who spent the better part of his time being in love with others.

Sometimes she fell in love with other people; she found interesting ways to express it. "I had a French friend here once that Dorothy was mad for," former art consultant John Abbott recalls. "My French friend loved America, and American things, including Wonder Bread. Dorothy came over. We all drank a great deal. I woke up one morning and Dorothy was on the kitchen floor, her purse around her arm, her skirt hiked up, with a trail of Wonder Bread leading to her cunt. Uneaten."

Sometimes she wrote letters. In one letter she wrote: "God knows where I will go next. (Death?) Do you have any plans?"

Sometimes she wrote detailed descriptions of the time she had spent in Holland and Belgium, long ago, for friends who were planning to visit both: "Avoid at all costs jaunts to Marken or Volendam—these are hideous holes kept up for tourist traffic; the inhabitants (ugliest people in the world because they all inter-marry and inter-breed) loiter about in colorful (sic) peasant garb, and that's all there is. . . . Chocolates in Belgium marvelous."

Sometimes she called herself these names: Black Bar-

barella, the Brown Recluse, the Tiny Recluse, the Brown Wren, Mother.

Sometimes she kept lists of words and phrases that she used in her work as a copy editor. Some of the words and phrases she wrote down were: appurtenances, teeming, infelicitous, verbal scrimmage, decorative function, colorless yokels, all too obvious, pauperize, inharmonious.

And as New York became an "out" city, "Scumsville" attracted an ever-increasing influx of gay men from other parts of the country Dean would never know. The parameters of her world were expanding. The gossip and secrets she had once traded no longer amused everyone; she no longer knew who "everyone" was. "In 1974 fag hags [of my generation] became obsolete," recalls Penny Arcade in her performance piece "Bitch! Dyke! Fag Hag! Whore!" "It was all about sex for gay men. Things got so bad I had to start talking to other fag hags."

And in order to wrest a semblance of control over her rapidly growing world, Dean helped make certain private intrigues public, outing herself in more ways than one in the process.

The "Bronfman kidnapping" first made the newspapers in August 1975, when it was reported that Sam Bronfman II had been abducted from the driveway of his mother's house in Purchase, New York, by three unidentified men. Sam Bronfman, aged twenty-one, was a nephew of Arthur Loeb and the eldest son of Edgar Bronfman, then the head of the Seagram Company, a billion-dollar enterprise. Edgar Bronfman agreed to pay millions in ransom, and deposited the money at the designated place and time—in Queens at three in the morning. But Sam was not released.

Two days later, as the result of a tip, he was found, unharmed, in an apartment house in Brooklyn; the money was discovered in an apartment in a nearby building. Had the whole thing been staged with Sam's help?

Sam denied knowing anyone connected with the incident. But for those inclined to be suspicious of the kidnapping, Dean's associations provided some intriguing clues. According to people who knew her at the time, Dean claimed that several months before the incident took place she had introduced Sam to Willie Dunn, a former friend of Arthur Loeb's. It has been suggested that she helped Willie Dunn devise the scenario for Sam's abduction. In any case, she seemed to know all the major participants. It has also been suggested that, to stage the kidnapping, Dunn enlisted the help of two friends, a firefighter and a limousine-service operator. (Although these two men were later indicted for kidnapping, they were ultimately acquitted of the charge and convicted only of grand larceny.) Currently, Sam is professionally subordinate to his younger brother, Edgar Bronfman, Jr., the president and CEO of Seagram.

"Somehow it got leaked to a number of people or papers that Dorothy was involved," Peter Prescott says. "She was afraid to stay in her apartment after that, so she came to stay with me for a while. She was distraught. She kept saying, 'I know too much, I know too much.' "

Perhaps Dean's involvement with Bronfman was a response to the bitterness she felt over the way in which Arthur Loeb had ended their friendship. Or perhaps it had begun as a joke, the way most things used to in the gay environs of New York. But that world had changed; and with it, Dean's position of authority. Her eccentricities became greater. She saw fewer and fewer members of the original Brotherhood, most of whom had gone on to careers, to AA, or to steady lovers. She continued (sporadically) to produce *The All-Lavender Cinema Courier*, but the low camp of its language and wit belonged to another time, a different generation: "*Exorcist II: The Heretic.* Woe betide the naïf who elects to squander gay pennies and/or time on this large scale clinker. Sequel to you know what . . . Yet know the by now renascent dedemonized Linda Blair, about 18, gelatinous of texture, and to all intents and purposes well-primed in the arts of tap dancing, polyestered harlotry (viz., massive, flopping boobs; puffy countenance; sluttish makeup; platform shoes such as worn only by hookers and members of minority groups, be the latter down-or-up-trodden), is an outpatient at a flashy psychiatric clinic . . ."

"*Murder by Death.* Murder of audience by dearth of amusement would be more telling a title. Why bother to 'spoof'—that awful word again—a genre so empty as that of the detective story? All the famous stars on hand are utterly gone to waste, and it is disheartening to see them reduced to such low circumstances. As for that petulant pansy Truman Capote—hopelessly non-professional and entirely the fat dowdy frump, though I am sure he thinks he is terribly, terribly sophisticated. Don't waste any gay pennies on this one, despite all the advt. campaign." Dean kept scrapbooks filled with images of pandas and koala bears. In 1975, she wrote a letter to the marketing division of Buitoni, correcting their use of Italian on a jar of spaghetti sauce, and elicited this response: "Dear Ms. Dean:

Thank you very much for taking the time and interest to bring to our attention the erroneous spelling of Correggio on the back panel of the Eggplant Parmigiana . . . To express our appreciation, enclosed please find a coupon good for $2.00 toward your next Buitoni Frozen Food purchase. . . ." She developed an obsession with Clint Eastwood: "Gentlemen: I wish to inquire as to whether United Artists is contemplating a Manhattan re-release of *Thunderbolt and Lightfoot*," she wrote to the publicity department. "If not, why not? If so, when and where? Preferably immediately at a theater into which a female might safely venture unescorted."

In an attempt to have her upstairs neighbors evicted, she kept a detailed report of their activities, which she claimed prevented her from "working."

15 June 1978. Thursday

Afternoon—restless shuffling, pacing in place (Dining Area)

Banshee wails from the kitchen

16 June 1978. Friday

ca. 8:15 pm DITTO, with more banshee wailing random stumbling, jousting, jostling, roaring (vacuum cleaner—which is always flung down, rather than put down), stomping . . .

17 June 1978. Saturday

Wailing, furniture scraping

Her attempts evidently failed. Before long, she herself was evicted. "Am exceedingly demoralized and depressed in the face of so much dishonesty, sneakiness, malice, stupidity on the other side," she wrote of her neighbors, after she had taken them to court. "To say nothing of their willfulness, petulance, crassness, etc., etc. To have to defend one's actions in the interests of self-preservation before such a collection of scumbags as these staggers the moral imagination, to put it mildly." Raymond Sokolov, the arts editor of *The Wall Street Journal*, recalls: "When Dorothy was thrown out of Morton Street, she was convinced she was going crazy. I took her to St. Vincent's so she could get treatment, dry out. She hated the doctor—he wore an earring in one ear. After he'd examined her, he said that Dorothy must be delusional: 'She keeps saying she went to Radcliffe.'"

She kept a journal for a time detailing her medical problems.

4 Feb:

Night—numbness, tingling in feet, legs first noticed. The cold weather?

9 Mar:

Morning—that it has palpably worsened, to the point of being virtually incapacitating. Am instructed/advised by Dr. Louis Scarrone, RE-7-6868, to consult St. Vincent Clinic (not emergency ward).

A.M. 15 March (Thurs):

"Half-deafness" provoked by jammed-in ear plug the night before. Through the day—feeling that whole left side of face (eye), maybe more, approaching "paralysis."

19 Ma 1200–530:

Findings uncertain. Malnutrition?

Her drinking increased and she wouldn't join AA. "Everyone I knew who joins gets so boring," she said. "I went to my first AA meeting today," she said to another friend. "Let's have a drink."

In 1973, she had become a bouncer at Max's Kansas City, the legendary rock club in Union Square. Sitting on a stool, her legs dangling, she didn't need a velvet rope to keep people out. Her withering glance told people to stay away. In a poem entitled "Dear Dorothy (for Dorothy Dean)," the poet Robert Creeley wrote:

> *I get scared of getting*
> *lost, I hold on hard*
> *to you. Your voice was*
> *instantly familiar.*

Creeley met Dean in 1973, and recalls a "very pleasant afternoon spent drinking" at Max's. He says: "About five-thirty, Dorothy had to leave. We were both a little wobbly. And as she made her way to the great swinging doors, I undertook to help her, whereupon she swung at me with her great leather purse, growling, 'Fuck off, you creep!' And I understood what she meant: that I had presumed she needed help, and—an even greater presumption—that I thought I could be the one to offer it."

Soon afterward, she fell in love with Norman Fischer, who sold cocaine to art-world luminaries such as Sam Wagstaff, and his boyfriend at the time, photographer Robert Mapplethorpe. She called Fischer "the Forbidden Fruit." In a joint letter to Frick Museum curator Edgar Munhall and John Abbott, Dean wrote: "Just to Keep You up to date on the ROMANCE of my wan life. On Monday evening, 7 June last (a date graven in memory for all eternity), I actually had, at his suggestion, a real live honest-to-god date with the Forbidden Fruit. We went to a little opera at Alice Tully Hall (during the performance I actually got to hold the FF's hand, it was indescribably thrilling) . . . Unfortunately, the evening fell apart when we returned to the Forbidden Fruitstand [and] . . . a whole swarm of that riff-raff and trash with which Norman . . . is wont to associate invaded the fairy aerie . . . Anyway, privacy and intimacy quickly dissipated, and I left in tears." (Norman Fischer was one of the first men to die of AIDS in New York, in 1979.)

She kept detailed lists of her expenses in neat columns: "Mar 1 'Lunch': 5.08. Reference books: 10.16. Entertaining A. DeGroat: 23. Legal Aid—MTA 1. Bounced check: 4. Chain smoking [no cost mentioned]. Coffee intake [no cost mentioned]. Increased electricity bills (working at night) [no cost mentioned]."

She became socially more difficult. She became disoriented and unmanageable when she drank. "Dear D. Dean," the actor and former Warhol superstar Taylor Meade wrote. "Thanks for your letter. The evening at Sardi's was delicious. You behaved with the utmost soigné until . . . in the cab home you kept telling the driver he was going in the wrong direction and that you didn't like him. Mildly embarrassing. Love." In 1979, when Dean was forty-six, she applied to Harvard Law School, writing in her application: "I feel so strongly on the subject of civilized surroundings that, even if rejected by Harvard Law School, I am resolved next fall to move back . . . to

Cambridge. It is psychologically and ethically familiar, intellectually and behaviorally congenial, which New York
City emphatically is not."

In her application to law school, she also wrote: "Here
it is expedient, perhaps, to comment on one obstacle mentioned which I have *not* successfully overcome, and that
is the economic. To this moment, I remain . . . as poor as
a churchmouse, relative to the standards of my coevals
with similar educational advantages. It is extremely difficult to pinpoint the valid explanation for this, but most
probably it has to do in a general sense with the fact that
(for whatever reasons) I have never, until now, been pos-
sessed of any specific driving ambition whose achievement
might have resulted in palpable monetary gain. The
proper focus for my 'capabilities' or 'talents' or what you
will has eluded me in the past. Until now, I have never
been conscious of any line of work to which I was whole-
heartedly interested in committing my intellectual re-
sources fully. (In all honesty, I must add that I personally
do not feel—and I may, of course, be wrong—that being
female and being Negro have in the long run proved anywhere near so detrimental to my economic advancement
as had the above-mentioned factor [though possibly the
three are interdependent]. This assuredly has not been the
situation relative to, say, that of my mother and others of
her generation. Nonetheless, if the attributes 'female' and
'black' abstractly are to be considered assets [if only for
statistical purposes] in the eyes of the Admissions Committee, I sincerely hope these will be emphasized accord-
ingly.)"

Instead, in 1980, at the invitation of a friend, Dean

moved to Boulder, Colorado, another college town, ostensibly to stop drinking. "John Barleycorn is still a close acquaintance, though," she wrote to John Abbott. "From the sound of it, you yourself have become overly friendly with the same. Beware. Much of my present trouble has arisen through [its] sad discovery. . . . Did I tell you about the local phenomenon, the Liquor Mart? This place occupies a sweep of approx. 18 city blocks, liquor, liquor everywhere . . ." In Boulder, which she liked because "there is no Art and there is no Fashion—this is an enormous relief," she supported herself working in a bookstore and then as a copy editor and proofreader. She stopped drinking from time to time. She even occasionally attended Bible classes, as though she were trying to become the girl she had never been: docile, polite, the daughter of a man of vision.

She never pursued the whereabouts of the child she had given up for adoption—a talisman of the past. She returned to "Scumsville" primarily for funerals. There were fewer and fewer calls put through to her Central Swishboard. So many people she had known were getting ready to be sick or dying, and so was the subculture of which she had been a part. On return trips to New York, she witnessed what her fictional contemporary, Odette O'Doyle, describes in James McCourt's *Time Remaining*: "You've heard me on ACT/OUT, Aggrieved Children Throwing One Uncut Tantrum . . . All [they] want is . . . recognition and vindication on the primary narcissistic level."

Dean never abandoned language; she wrote many letters to old friends who had given her up or had already become sick or died. Sometimes her letters were roundabout requests for money to install a telephone or to buy new reading glasses. She didn't often ask for pity, but when she did it was on her own terms, and phrased as a joke. What some people would remember most about Dorothy was her smile. Robert Creeley wrote, in his poem "Dear Dorothy (for Dorothy Dean)":

> *Your ineluctable*
> *smile, it falls back in your head,*
> *your smile with such a gentle*
> *giving up*

Seven years before her death, Dean wrote to Abbott: "Well, I'ze tired. I hope you eventually get this letter and eventually (before it is too late) will answer it. In the meantime, have fun. You know how; I don't anymore."

3

Put the niggers over there, he said, indicating one of his white floor-to-ceiling bookcases that was literally littered with niggers, or what he referred to as "niggerati," a term invented by the folklorist and writer Zora Neale Hurston. And "niggerati" was how the poet, novelist, playwright, and instructor Owen Dodson used to describe the Negro fag intellectuals whose reflexive, sentimental race consciousness comprised much of the aesthetics and the ideology that informed the Harlem Renaissance.

The books written by the men and women Owen referred to as "niggerish," and whom he asked me to put "over there," had been published in the twenties, thirties, and forties; those books had gone the way many literary vogues do—abandoned on someone's dusty shelf, book jackets tattered, with personal inscriptions as faint as the faint ideas expounded in them. In Owen's youth, the literary vogue had focused on the "New Negro," his or her "story." The aesthetic of the New Negro celebrated, in folklore and poetry, novels and plays, these authors' misbegotten Southern or Middle American pasts along with their eventual brief stardom in that colored mecca known as Harlem. The philosopher Alain Locke, who coined the phrase "New Negro," wrote in 1925: "There is ample evidence of a New Negro in the latest phases of social change and progress, but still more in the internal world of the Negro mind and spirit." The New Negro writers' internal worlds were never revealed in their work, which did not examine their abiding intellectual and emotional curiosity about European culture; nor did it speak of their aspiration to be absorbed by that culture, where they would find new privilege as the objects of curiosity. Nor did their work examine the deeper exigencies of the mind, the self. The work of New Negro writers such as Zora Neale Hurston, Langston Hughes, Alain Locke, and Countee Cullen—all of whom Owen had known—did not explain why or how they had adopted "race" as a frame for their work; it did not explain how they constructed that frame out of fear—the fear that, should they be divested of rhetoric, they would no longer exist—or, at the very least, risked being absorbed by the existential debate that consumes every writer: Who Am I? Instead, they chose ideology, the sanctimonious: As a Black, I Am, or Was, or Should Be.

As New Negroes, they defended their right to be "oppressed"; as agents of the rhetoric of oppression, they were insistent on their "correctness." Often this position resulted in bad prose and (far more often) bad poetry. The New Negro supported the continuum of white power by bemoaning, on the page, its existence. And for this performance, the New Negroes were roundly applauded by white publishers and patrons, who rewarded them with stipends, book deals, and no criticism whatsoever. What the New Negro was: a model of repressed and repressive colored middle-class aspirations.

These New Negroes were children hungry for the comfort of group ideology (or therapy). They sought validation everywhere, even as they took up their pens to inscribe feebly in those now forgotten books: "To Our Brother, Owen Dodson." Knowing all of this but not voicing it, Owen said *Put the niggers over there* with irony. He said it to those critics and scholars whom he eyed with disdain because they took the period's infantile cultural production seriously, and because they remained willfully ignorant of the Harlem Renaissance's true significance: as the moment when Negro social life devolved from Negro to black.

I met Owen Dodson, this collector of traces of Negro social life of the thirties and forties, through a woman friend of his whom he had known since high school, and who was also a friend of my mother's. For a fee, this woman taught poetry and piano to "gifted" children interested in either. I got a scholarship. I didn't study poetry there; instead I studied the woman's matted wig, her bad teeth, and her intractable bewilderment: her bewilderment over her continued connection to her husband, who had gone blind during the war after refusing to be treated with penicillin for syphilis; her bewilderment over not being able to manage the mean and hungry dogs she kept locked in an attic; her bewilderment over young people like myself, whose ambition would consume what she had to offer and carry them on to the next person they would need to consume in order to become something other than themselves. This woman said: I want to send you to my friend Owen's house; he wants to give away books. I was thirteen then. It was 1974.

On the afternoon we first met, Owen showed me a number of photographs that had been taken of him when he was young. Through these photographs, I was able to see how much I resembled him. We also resembled one another in our ability to charm, and in what we falsely projected: relatively easy access to our internal selves. In order to be liked, we had both learned how to please an audience. By the time I met Owen, he was said to have become exhausted by his charm. In order to be charming, he drank, and drink energized him socially, unless he drank too much, which was most of the time. At the time, I had just begun to be confused by my attraction to reflection (writing) and to being social. We were in love at first sight.

He took the American Negro's xenophobic interest in my West Indian background. I took an interest in his connection to Negro glamour and social life. I learned that afternoon that much of Negro social custom had been built on skewered European social mores—in the overlaying of European formality of dress with visual rhetoric (the oversized tiger lily attached to the lapel in place of a discreet boutonniere; the heavily pomaded hair instead of a crisp bob). I also learned that the principle of Negro style was "making do," and then flaunting it. This was all as disjunctive and foreign to me as the images I had seen of moneyed Chinese wearing European dress during the twenties.

Two years after that, my ambition found me a frequent visitor to Owen's home carrying out his command to *Put* *the niggers over there*, in the bookcase opposite his bed. There was dust on the books. His lips were like impacted dust. When he said *Put the niggers over there*, he pointed with a long, crooked finger with a blunt nail—his left index finger—which was heavy with one silver ring, indicating where the books should be put. I put the niggerish books on the shelf. I was fifteen. Already I knew that the India-ink inscriptions—"To Owen Dodson, cher maître" and so on—were the faded sentiments of friends he had not seen for many years. But the impulse to befriend and to garner the respect of students had not faded enough from his memory for him to resist his impulse to nurture other people, other writers. He was a pedant. He could not trust his mind to isolation.

The dim yellow light filled with dust motes circled next to the nigger books whose inscriptions trembled with age. To one side of the bookcase were letters stored in letter boxes from many people he used to amuse, people who no longer received him socially since he had been crippled by arthritis and had had two hip operations. He was incoherent half the time. His small hand with its blunt nail curled around the necks of liquor bottles. Sometimes, after waking, or when he was ready to receive students, his hand also wrapped around the necks of Listerine bottles, still in their green wrappers. He gargled in the vain hope that Listerine would make his tongue and teeth desirable to all the young men who would never allow Owen to call them lover, many of whom pitied his shrunken, heavily cologned figure just enough to allow his gray-haired head to graze their young and wide-with-ambition shoulders, but never enough to let his hand graze their crotches.

By the time I met him, he rarely said what he thought. Nor did he think much before he spoke. His speech was reflexive and articulate but not necessarily thoughtful. He was slowly turning into a dust mote. Often he bounced happily on the air expelled by the laughter of friends and hangers-on, or of loyal former students from Howard University, where he had been head of the university's Drama Department. He told many of the same stories many times. He told how, after he had committed himself to directing the first production ever of James Baldwin's *The Amen Corner*, at Howard in 1954 ("The deans said, 'This play will put the Speech Department back fifty years!'"), Baldwin arrived in Washington for the premiere and quickly encamped himself in Owen's home, followed by his lover, and his enormous family, who proceeded to eat Owen out of house and home. "Niggers!" Owen exclaimed at the end of this story, which was meant to illustrate his own character, his tale of kindnesses unpaid, debts tallied. His dusty lips began to flake as he reached to pour himself another drink and another story.

Once I put my tongue in his mouth after he had vomited into his soup plate during a dinner he had prepared with the help of his older sister, Edith, with whom he lived. The dinner was in honor of the many colored people who still considered Owen's home on West Fifty-first Street a landmark of Negro style. The people I saw there were the actors Roscoe Lee Brown and Ruby Dee and Ossie Davis;

the novelists Margaret Walker and Toni Morrison ("She
was Howard's beauty queen one year!"), and others he
would eventually put "over there" on the shelf. Vomiting
into his soup plate, he sputtered and choked while his
guests pretended not to notice, as did Edith, who was
smaller than her brother and more suspicious. She suf-
fered from a sexual despair that was the result of a first
marriage gone bad and her self-perceived homeliness,
which endowed her with the patience and moral fortitude
necessary to read John Galsworthy's *The Forsyte Saga*
over and over again, as well as an ability to ignore her
brother's repeated emotional indiscretions: the way he elevated every male student to protégé and, eventually, to
husband.

I took the plate swimming with Listerine and liquor and
soup remains and flushed it down the toilet. He moved
away from the table. He had a walker, a silver walker that
helped him *clink clunk* down the endless red-carpeted hall-
way, its walls hung with one large painting of San Sebas-
tián and one large drawing of Icarus falling; these images
represented his literary imagination, just as the wooden
posters cramming the dining-room walls, announcing per-
formances long past—Katharine Cornell in *The Doctor's
Dilemma* and Charles Trenet on Columbia Records—represented his attachment to grand theater and bohemian-
ism.

Although many, many people knew what Owen's intellectual and aesthetic tastes were, they never discussed
the absence of those tastes from his written work, where
he forfeited his vision for the sake of Negro respect-
ability, writing what he felt should be said instead of

what he wanted to say, as in his "Poem for Pearl's Dancers":

> *On my back they've written history, Lord,*
> *On my back they've lashed out hell. . . .*
> *When my children get to reading, Lord,*
> *On my back they'll read my tale.*

Such sentiments were literally employable. In 1947, he served as the executive secretary for the Committee for Mass Education in Race Relations, intended to help "abolish" Hollywood's stereotypical view of blacks. He was anthologized in *The Book of Negro Folklore*, edited by Langston Hughes, in 1958. Because, by the time I met him, most of his friends were his former students, he never admitted how lost he was when he wrote. In his second novel, *Come Home Early, Child*, written in 1958 but not published until 1977, Owen's characters shrink beneath the glare of the greasepaint he rubs on their cheeks for effect. He was too lazy intellectually to look for the metaphors best suited to express his meaning in his poems, plays, or novels; he relied instead on hackneyed "poetic" language to create character.

His work was an interesting example of a tired genre; it was the product of a *deliberately* "black" writer whose primary talent was spent seeking out an audience to view the chip on his shoulder, a chip darker than the author himself. Owen wrote:

Slaves: (laughing)
Ya gonna discover one of these days

That the white man got two dozen ways to lie an cheat
To conjure with deceit.

Many of the poems that appear in his first collection, *Powerful Long Ladder* (1946), imitated the dialect his white predecessors had used in their work, poets such as Edgar Lee Masters and Carl Sandburg. Owen's imitations of those poets who appropriated black syntax—itself a linguistic metaphor for the outsiderness they felt—was as ill-fitting as Uncle Jimbilly's woolly, unconditional love and speech in Katherine Anne Porter's short story "The Witness." It is difficult to account for the poems Owen wrote in dialect: he was born and raised in Brooklyn. But dialect he used, hoping to become authentic in his "blackness" rather than distinct in his Negroness. From "Black Mother Praying":

Listen, Lord, they ain't nowhere for black mothers to
   turn
Won't you plant your son's goodness in this land
Before it too late?
Set your stars of sweetness twinklin' over us like winda
   lamps
Before it too late?

By the time I met him, he was no longer interested in writing. He had already begun to move away from the expansive interior places writing could have taken him to. He was interested in people, the social life his "name" generated, and in representing those parts of his style he could still access through his flirtatious and "exotic" clothes.

In the twilight blue of his room, Owen collapsed on his bed; he had one "real" hip and one large shoe with a lift in it. I took off his brocaded vest and then turned on his bedside lamp; gravity pulled his brown skin back; his face was suddenly as smooth as a death mask. There was the smell of urine in his bed. A bottle clanked under the bed; he had been drinking alone before dinner, dust motes floating above him, and history floating above him too, which he could not keep out of his room, not even with the heavy drapes that covered the windows of his thirteenth-floor penthouse on West Fifty-first Street. Those curtains locked it in, like a neurasthenic's will. His apartment was located across from a town house to which was attached a neon sign that read, on one side: "Jesus Saves," and on the other: "Sin Will Find You Out." I removed the trousers and vest he had put on with great effort hours before, when, slumped in his bed, he had applied a hair tonic to smooth back his hair and comb his mustache. He made his wobbly way to the dinner table, where he told one story ("When Edith and I were little, we had to recite in church and quote the scriptures. Edith's quote: 'Jesus wept' ") before throwing up in his plate and making his way back to the bed and reaching up for my face and kissing my mouth, whispering, "Do what you want," in my ear, just as I started unbuttoning his shirt. The bedroom door was slightly ajar. I closed it and bent over him and put my tongue in his mouth, as happy for this moment of displeasure as I was happy for every moment of pleasure. His teeth clenched as I clenched his arms. I was

fifteen. He was older than my mother but just as committed to the experience of pain as she was, just as resolute
in his commitment to the internal visions the experience
of pain affords. Lying with him in this way, I heard my
mother's voice—my imagination's radio—and began to
understand that what I could give to Owen in moments
like these I would never live long enough to use in support
of my mother: my monstrous ambition, which she had no
interest in, but which accounted, in part, for my being
with Owen. With Owen, I was farther into the world than
my mother and sisters had ever been. Also: his home dis-
placed—momentarily—the bright and functional squalor
I lived in, but did not sacrifice the narrative of oppression
that inspired poems like Owen's "Black Mother Praying."
For years I emulated the ideology that served as the
poem's foundation: the search for a secular God, a God
theologian James Cone has called a "god of the oppressed." In Owen's arms, I learned many things. I learned
how to think. When I began thinking, he grew angry, because it wasn't long before I found out the sin in his work:
his inability to convey intimacy. He bypassed his own
individual experience for the *gemütlich* feel of group oppression. In his work he was not an individual but part of
a movement.

But within movements, hierarchies exist. As one of the
disenfranchised, Owen was less popular than his bête
noire, James Baldwin, in whose work one finds the pathos
that accounts for the continued popularity of Charles
Dickens' *David Copperfield* and *Oliver Twist*. Baldwin's
Notes of a Native Son simply places the articulate Dick-

ensian orphan in thrall to a black god—Father with his
inherited power to "oppress": "In my mind's eye I could
see [my father], ... hating and fearing every living soul
including his children who had betrayed him, too, by
reaching toward the world which had despised him. ... I
began to wonder what it could have felt like for such a
man to have had nine children whom he could barely
feed." It was galling for Owen to know that Baldwin began writing one of his most widely anthologized essays,
Notes of a Native Son, in Owen's home, fortified by Ow-
en's liquor and attention. And it would have upset Owen
to know that the one book of his that I borrowed and
never returned was Baldwin's *Nobody Knows My Name*,
in which he writes about his relationship with his mentor,
Richard Wright. I liked the book less for what Baldwin
had to say than for its dust jacket. The jacket showed
Baldwin through the grid of a broken window standing in
a pile of inner-city rubble. He projects a look of pathos
meant to chip away at the invulnerability of the general
reader. I have always been mesmerized by how writers
manage to theatricalize their isolation for the camera. Perhaps he appropriated this look of defenseless reason from
the work of Harlem Renaissance writers. I do know that
the poet Countee Cullen had been an instructor of Baldwin's at De Witt Clinton High School. In "Alas Poor Richard," Baldwin states: Wright's "work was an immense
liberation and revelation for me. He became my ally, and
my witness, and alas! my father."

I did not consider Owen my father, and his work was
not an immense liberation for me. What I loved and ad-

mired in Owen was his ability to project himself larger than any actor I had ever seen and to hurtle me back to the forties, the years of his greatest social success. When Owen took me to one restaurant or another that had been popular during the era, he would order a repast that had been chic then: shrimp cocktails and martinis. I especially loved being with him those nights, in that frozen time, which had occurred long before our friendship began. Eating with Owen was like eating his curiously shaped history. Like most great teachers, he opened up the world for me. Like most people, he resented it when I left him to find what I could in it.

I entered Owen's mouth and his liquor-swollen tongue made a sound against mine. He was grateful for my size, which embarrassed me—I was bigger but tried to walk small, talk small, leave the room without being in it, because I hated being physically larger than my admiration for him, which was considerable; also, my large body seemed like too obvious a metaphor for my ambition, which was also considerable.

But to his mind, my size made me a man in relation to his woman, his quivering vulnerability and position on the bed, which was one of acceptance. In the years since then, I learned to distrust others' acceptance of me; it only leads me to question what my own vulnerability might mean. In any case, being larger, I was immediately thought of by Owen, and in years to come, by many others, as forceful, someone whose sole physical purpose is to enter their body of acceptance again and again, becoming the spine that encloses closeness and encases intimacy; and there we were, with my spine bent over his breathing, like the spine of a tent, his skin like the folds of a tent. He was my first woman.

He did not say what he thought about this moment, or any other. He was always ambivalent about using language to describe sexual pleasure. He had despised his body from his earliest years as the youngest child of a family that had been considered one of Brooklyn's finest. His father, Nathaniel, had been a journalist, editor of the syndicated weekly *Afro-American Page*. But his family dissolved quickly when he was still a boy, due to the early deaths of his parents. By the time he was an adolescent, he had lost five brothers and sisters and was left with only two older sisters, Edith and Lillian, and his much beloved brother Kenneth. Lillian, the oldest, was stern in her Negro reverence of education and discipline. She supported her siblings on her schoolteacher's salary. She wore sensible shoes, the sound of her heels clacked in his head forever. He was especially close to his brother Kenneth ("I should have slept with him; we loved each other so"), but Kenneth died young ("When he died, I lay in a darkened bedroom; I screamed"). The entire family was stunned by their individual sexual despair; in a way they were sexual liars. Kenneth's death fueled Owen's romanticism. As such, he was impatient with intellection, or any process that intruded on the drama he erected around dying—"Sorrow is the only faithful one," he once wrote. He generally preferred imagining death even to physical intimacy. Kenneth had been the true romantic or a poet—Owen said.

Owen reached up and circled my neck with his hands. I lifted him slightly and bit both nipples on his chest. *Put the niggers over there*, he said, perhaps not thinking. So little in those niggerish books was the result of thinking. That language was produced for an audience, not for the writers themselves. This is what Owen surrounded himself with and one reason (maybe) why he spoke without thinking.

He went to Bates College in Maine, and received his master of fine arts degree in theater from Yale. After Yale: various teaching appointments before becoming a professor at Howard, where he staged Ibsen and got grants and so forth, and was so seemingly welcoming of talents greater than his own—the composer David Amram, Baldwin, et al.—that he filled himself up with more company and fewer words. His books of poetry—*The Confession Stone* and *Powerful Long Ladder*—and novels—*Boy at the Window, Come Home Early, Child*—and plays—*The Confession Stone, Divine Comedy*—are less about matching words to thoughts than about filling up his résumé and the ghastly vacuum of Negro achievement. He was filled up with—what? My tongue, from time to time. "Oh," he said as I tried to remove his one large shoe— enjoying the visual incongruity of things: one big shoe off, the normal shoe still on. Dust motes flew as his fingers fluttered around my face. Behind those fingers I thought: *One day, I will be as old as he is now, with someone who cares as little or as much as I do now.* For as long as I knew him (I left him when I was nineteen) our relationship was that of the pedant and his student consumed with ambition. What the pedant knows: his ambitious student will stop at nothing in order to learn how to be himself; he will stop at nothing, not even at inhaling his teacher's vomit-smeared breath, as penance for the guilt he feels in wanting this more than anything else: to become a self without the burden of the pedant's influence.

When I went to visit Owen the second or third or eighth time, he said, "I love you," a statement filled with thought or nonthought, which, moments later, made me want to throw myself in front of a subway train, an interestingly extreme response to his relatively innocuous declaration, a response which made me more interested in him. Let's think now: the blunt nail, the blunt ring, foot crippled by arthritis, red sheets. Was there blood on the sheets? My eyes play tricks on memory.

Entering his mouth with my tongue was like entering the atmosphere of another age, his breath an asphyxiating growth to which were attached musty books inscribed in now fading India ink; costumes he had saved from past productions; framed watercolors by former lovers (the artists Charles Sebree and St. Clair Christmas); a plethora of clothes and mementos stiff with the dry rot of age or curling in a dim sun obscured by gray clouds, as if left to the elements. Entering his mouth was like entering his apartment on West Fifty-first Street on autumn afternoons where one might find the poet Derek Walcott in a black turtleneck, his dark hair and light eyes already brilliant with future success and the reverence of his European colleagues; or the actress Ruby Dee, who suffocated any and all public space with her air of beleaguered "goodness"; or the writer Ed Bullins, whose plays Owen had staged at Howard and whom Owen categorized as a "nigger" because he envied Bullins' narcissistically induced success.

The reflection and isolation required to produce writing, good, bad, or indifferent, had never been as important to Owen as being liked. "I like you," he said, his breath shouting up into my face like the stale air drummed up by a million dull moths. Visiting him in that apartment, I saw an interesting decorating principle at work—loneliness was at its core; and it was overlaid with the style of the thirties, which was more Negro than black.

His apartment was also filled with illness, sexual despair, a propensity to be rhetorical, a talent to amuse. In photographs taken during his adolescence, the image he presented to the world was one of a slightly small-shouldered confidence—shirts with starched collars and a thin, vulnerable neck. When I looked at these photographs, carefully preserved and cherished in his family photo albums, I always saw his loneliness in the position of his neck. Later, after he began stacking illness up around him, he supported his largish head with the help of his right hand. In those later photographs, that hand blocks our view of his neck.

Besides his thin neck, he had: small feet and distended hips, one of which was artificial. He also had a fondness for thinly sliced cheese, weighty silver jewelry, and a vague dislike of women, at least sexually. He competed with women sexually for what he desired: a man—which he did not consider himself to be. Women were interesting to him as performers, since they could project in any number of plays he could direct what he could project with me only in the dark: his desire to be overcome by a force bigger than his "personality." There was his personality, there were the dust motes, and there I was, his one good leg wrapped around my waist, his trousers pulled down to his knees, perhaps thinking (he did not say): *And after this beloved, another and another.* But he did not say that; I'm imagining that for him now, since this is my story, finally, or, rather, a story I fight to own, since it is not independent of any and all of the people I have known, their shared gestures of intimacy or remorse, his leg wrapped around my waist as the dust motes circled my eyes, which reflected the gravity that pulled his face down around his pillow.

I have always hated to observe things, always, because to observe anything has meant I will remember it, and I have only wanted to experience Fidelity, Love, and Loss, in order to leave them all behind, and move on to the next experience. For some of us, each "fresh wave of consciousness is poison," as Marianne Moore wrote, and I knew, as I began to remove my shoes and socks—it was dark whenever we were together sexually; he preferred the lights off; and before the lights were turned out, he shuttered his eyes—that I needed him as much as he needed me, it was my first experience of love—and of the will I have sometimes exercised in avoiding it.

Sometimes, I heard the sound of birds on his terrace as our tongues became softer and softer toward each other in the experience of pleasure, as student and teacher, child and adult, man and woman—whatever. The birds, I imagined, were pigeons, steel gray like the night sky and the city itself, onto which his apartment door opened.

His apartment was a way station for personal mythologizing; in it, the personal history of celebrities was evoked. He said: "Chile, Mrs. Patrick Campbell always had the last word in her plays. She was appearing in Ibsen's *Ghosts*. In *Ghosts*, the son has the last word. On opening night, people waited expectantly to see what Mrs. Campbell would do. The curtain was going down. Her son in the play says his last words: 'Give me the sun, Mother, the sun.' The curtain was almost down. Mrs. Campbell said: 'No.' "

He said: "Chile, I met Billie Holiday through my boyfriend, Karl Priebe, in the forties. She was appearing in a club in New York, on Fifty-second Street. I came up from Washington to see Karl. He was working, and he suggested I come along to meet her. Chile, she was in this awful dressing room, smaller than my small bathroom. She called me 'Teach.' Her dress was hiked up around her waist. She was fanning her pussy with a fan. She said, looking straight at me, fanning her pussy: 'Teach, it's so goddamn hot in here.' "

He said: "Chile, Alain Locke was in love with Langston all those years, so long, the poor thing broke—he lost his mind. Alain was very close to his mother, you know. Anyway, Alain's mother finally died. But he couldn't bear to be separated from her. So he had her all dressed up and propped up in a chair. Then he had all the colored queens come over to take tea with his dead mother. He'd lead a queen over to where she sat, imperious, in her pearls, fortified by her son's filial devotion. 'Mother,' he'd say, 'you remember Owen,' and so on."

He said: "Chile, I went to see Esther Rolle as Lady Macbeth. She replaced all the 'thous' with 'dem' and 'dese.' Niggers!"

He said: "Chile, I saw Siobhan McKenna in Bernard Shaw's *Saint Joan*. All that beautiful English mixed up in that Irish brogue. When the crowd starts screaming: 'Burn her, burn her,' I wanted to get out of my seat and scream: 'Yes! Burn dirty bitch.' "

He said: "Chile, Auden was in love with me. But he wasn't attractive. He lent me his house on Ischia to write in—off-season. I was supposed to be writing. I couldn't for a long time. His presence was overwhelming. He wasn't *there* but he was overwhelming."

He was a marvel of gift giving. In his criticism—in the late seventies he began a series of pieces on the history of black theater for *Black American Literature Forum* that he never finished—his gentleness and sense of "correctness" took precedence over his judgment. He apologized for most things in this common world, including himself, by being solicitous of other people—and then faulting them for their lack of sensitivity. He apologized for his privately uttered forthright and funny criticism of the black theater of the sixties and seventies by writing criticism which relied heavily on poetic "effect" so as to avoid being critical. "I have made no conclusions, given no criteria for what a play is or should be," he wrote in

Black American Literature Forum. "The effect of a play is like the wind—an invisible wind that can nonetheless have an effect on the leaves and branches of our lives by its whisper, or rage, or its very stillness."

He made the world less common through exposing many people to many things they had never known before. He wrote to me once: "Chile, you must read Shakespeare, you must." He taught me what *mene, mene, tekel, upharsin* meant and who Eleonora Duse was. He made me read W. H. Auden's poem "Musée des Beaux Arts." He knew that I would be interested in *why* none of the villagers saw Icarus falling. He played a recording of Gertrude Stein's opera *Four Saints in Three Acts.* Through the scratches on the record, I saw the sound of words float above our heads.

What I also loved in Owen's apartment: the absence of Negro envy, which is to say the absence of envy professional Negroes feel toward one another everywhere. Owen dispelled it when he saw it in his home by being an example of its folly: here was a lonely Negro with cracked lips and wit who had more or less given up on trying to prove anything to anyone. He was competitive in one sense only: making joy as theatrical as possible. For him joy was artificial and hollow and meant the same thing as irony. Being ironic was valuable: it told life that you knew what it was up to.

The point is, I wanted to be as close to all this as possible—the glamour of creation—in order to write it down. Owen, on the other hand, preferred literary society to writing. In order to be closely associated with what he admired, he told stories about the great he had known marginally; if he could not be a great writer, he would have access to greatness. The men he had known as a boy, those who comprised the homosexual faction of the Harlem Renaissance, and who were considered "great," he became friends with. They were like him, at least on the surface: nattering, spinsterish, careful personalities who sacrificed wit on the page for that dry-mouthed abstraction known as the Negro cause.

They were stymied in their desire. Their deepest secrets were codified in poems like Countee Cullen's "To the Three for Whom the Book," in his collection *The Black Christ and Other Poems*, published in 1929:

> *Once like a lady*
> *In a silken dress*
> *The serpent might eddy*
> *Through the wilderness,*
> *Billow and glow*
> *And undulate*
> *In a rustling flow*
> *Of sinuous hate.*
> *Now dull-eyed and leaden,*
> *Of having lost*
> *His Eden*
> *He pays the cost. . . .*
> *But you three rare*
> *Friends whom I love . . .*
> *A book to you three*
> *Who have not bent*
> *The idolatrous knee. . . .*

Owen said: "Chile, one of the people Countee dedicated that poem to was his boyfriend, Harold Jackman, right after Countee decided he had to go straight and get married. I heard Harold's sister, Ivy, burned all those fabulous letters Countee sent."

The fags Owen had grown up admiring did not have direct access to their emotional lives. They built complete narratives around love they could not reciprocate unless that love was brief, experienced while on sabbatical or waylaid in a port in Naples. Instead of having relationships, they decorated their hearts and apartments in fabulous thirties style, a style that was a terrible joke on a world they assumed could take what they had to offer if they presented it in its correct form. The result: their "correct" sartorial sense—the bow ties and tweed suits of the English schoolmaster. They were never "dirty." They were never "incorrect." They kept their fingernails blunt. Their ability to suck up the dust motes of disturbance, anger, and bad feeling was admirable. The poet Patrick O'Connor, who was, for a time, Owen's roommate in Washington, D.C., in the early fifties, said to me once: "I loved being taught upper-class manners by a black person." They looked with some disdain on the personal hygiene of white faggots, whom they considered the worst thing imaginable, "nasty," although they coveted their "allure." Because of his eminence as a connoisseur of Negro fags among certain white English and European fags he loved recalling European and English fairies involved in the "arts," who used to call; the fag circuit was very small in the forties.

Owen arranged a tryst for a black friend whom the actor John Gielgud admired. "And how was it to sleep with one of the greatest living actors of this century?" Owen inquired of his friend the morning after. Owen's friend made a face. He said: "His drawers were shitty."

The women in my family affected respect for him. What the women in my family found difficult to respect was the fact that he was a man, influential in worlds they did not know. Nevertheless, he provoked feelings of jealousy in those women, since he was the first person of substance to claim my attention away from them. One sister in particular (the one most like me) criticized our relationship beyond recognition. She said: "He's turning my brother into a faggot." I remember how I tried to avoid my sister's scorn by not speaking of Owen, and how often I saw him, how often the dust floated around our joined lips. Early I learned that any personal information offered to powerful women was subject to becoming a narrative outside my control. They could not see me as a boy but only as a teenage girl—as their younger girl-selves, in effect. If I did not submit to their view of me, I would become part of a world they hated. I would become a man, replete with a narrative they could not access. In order to claim me back, they had to chip away at my friendship with Owen. They did so by planting disaster in the air, labeling me a faggot. I had been raised never to contradict women, particularly the women in my own family, even as they tried to kill me with insults as I moved outside their identity. It is only now that I attempt to slip past the identity they have established for me, as their younger sister, and into a narrative that, even as I write, rejects my intellection, my control, because I betrayed its central character so long ago: Owen. Back then, I did not say to my mother and sisters: I am already a faggot. I am not a woman. I am not you, but myself, which is what he perhaps loved in his bedroom then, my thin vulnerable chest, the nipples that moved when my bird arms moved. Owen understood my treachery because he knew what deference and fear of women meant; he knew I would give our friendship up for them. He accepted my betrayal as he accepted so much else, holding me in his arms, as I thought: *If I give him up, I will be embraced by the women I know who have yet to claim their lives.* The body alone does not make a woman, but a certain cast of mind does, that cast of mind that creates disaster even as it tries to withstand the disaster it has created. In his room, my lies closed in on me: I had lied by saying I would be with him forever. I lied because he had come to love so late. I knew then that I would come to love late in life as well, when I was no longer able to recognize it as such and had no need to avoid it. I had lied to my sisters and my mother when I told them I would no longer see him. And I caught myself in these lies so that I could disdain all of them for making me lie, and leave myself free to move away from them. That something other than myself I wanted to become had to be a someone who did not come from anywhere where women had the power to displace my love and confusion for men like Owen. I have yet to become that person. Lying there, his lips caked with regret and the need to please, Owen did not say: *He will leave me, as all students do.* He did not say: *You will be many things, a liar foremost, because lying will protect you from yourself.* He did not say: *Look and see what human interaction leads to: lying for convenience.* He clutched my bird arm tighter as I got up to leave. I was nineteen the last time we allowed this intimacy to happen between us. I was nineteen when I left him forever. He had three years to live and we would never speak again. In that moment, I resigned to make my way back to the women I presumed loved me and who would not let me go in a metaphysical sense, even though they would go on to other lives, with very little thought to what I had given up for them, for myself: my study of the larger world through this man, to whom I showed no mercy but every tenderness. As I put on my shirt, my naked back turned to him and my first experience of physical love, I was being the good boy I was brought up by women to be, the good boy Owen's sister Lillian had raised him to be, which is to say the kind of boy who would not contradict a woman's position in the world by examining who she was and asking himself what that might mean to him. Lillian's ghost hovered in the best poem Owen was to write, a poem that accompanied a book of photographs by James Van Der Zee called *The Harlem Book of the Dead.* It is comprised of images taken at funeral homes and at the mourners' homes; they are photographs of the living courting the dead. Owen's poem is six lines long. In it he says:

We grew so lonely knowing one another
Please was our only vocabulary

now and again
Will you be with me please
A word with a vegetable sound
Please

The photograph Owen's poem accompanied showed two coffins, which held a brother and sister. The poem was spoken from the mouth of the dead woman.